HUMAN CRYSTALS

Patricia Leahy-Shrewsbury

Foreword Copyright © Beverley Collett 2007

Book Cover Design: Ryan Morrison
www.cupcakedesigns.com.au

Editing: Margaret Johnson
ask@bookdoctor.com.au

To order more books contact:

Patricia Leahy-Shrewsbury
Email: pleahy-shrewsbury@bigpond.com
Website: www.pleahy-shrewsbury.com

Published by Ocean Publishing
Printed and bound in Western Australia
ISBN 978-1-920783-82-2

To my sons Adam and Craig
And my husband Roberto
With all my love and gratitude

Table of Contents

Cultural Sensitivity

Readers of Aboriginal heritage are warned that this book includes the name of an Aboriginal person who is now deceased. He was a traditional elder of the Ngarinyin Tribe. Every effort was made to contact his children in order to obtain their permission to include him in *Human Crystals*. Unfortunately, direct contact was never made in spite of Kevin Shaw's enquiries on my behalf. However, this elder has willingly had his name and photographs included in several other books about his life and the Dreamtime stories. I therefore, with the greatest respect, feel comfortable about naming him and including my photograph of the Wandjina in *Human Crystals*.

My valued friend and guide, who is an indigenous law-keeper, I have named Auntie to preserve her anonymity.

The organiser of the trip to the Kimberley region has asked that her name be changed; so in this story she is called Mary.

Acknowledgements

I would not have a story to tell were it not for the communication established with the blue light beings and angels. I am forever grateful for their practical guidance, unconditional love, and sense of humour.

Human Crystals was physically written thanks to Kathy Beardsell's generous donation of a computer and many hours of patiently teaching me how to use it.

Thank you to Margaret Johnson for her clear and valuable input editing *Human Crystals*. Thank you also to Helga Busch for her detailed proofreading.

I owe an enormous debt of gratitude to my husband Roberto Shrewsbury, Craig Loukes, Adam Loukes, Katie Busch, Maggie Hall, Beverley Collett, Flic Shooter, Wynelle Delaney, Susie Garratt, Sheahara, Diane Brice and all my friends and family for believing in me, sharing in the magic of our journey together, and being an indispensable part of my life.

This is a true account of the spiritual guidance I received and the adventures that ensued. When writing of people and events I can only describe them from my perspective. It is my intention to portray them in an honest and loving light.

Foreword

'You must be Bev,' she said, and I was fixed by her wide smile and clear blue eyes.

'And you're Patti.' Laughing, we hugged right there in the little general store in Nannup. We had been alerted by mutual contacts that we should meet. I had never set eyes on this woman before, but I knew her. The year was 1980. Patti, like myself, had embraced the New Age ethos of the 70s and had headed 'bush', seeking a simple lifestyle. Forming a friendship that seemed to transverse eons, we exchanged books and ideas.

These were days when new ideas sprouted like oats after the first autumn rains; however, at that time there were only two bookshops in Perth that stocked esoteric books, the Magic Circle and the Theosophical. We grasped books by Maxwell Maltz, Lyall Watson and Alan Toffler and others. Then along came Bill Mollison with Permaculture, and books on building your own home and growing organic vegies. The hole in the ozone layer was a whisper, but we listened. So we went back to basics.

We decided to start a personal development and meditation group in the Nannup town hall. Participants took turns to lead the group using exercises from Jean Houston's *The Possible Human* workbook, and were encouraged to share their particular expertise with us.

We invited informed speakers to visit Nannup and instruct us on Buddhism, Metamorphosis, yoga, various forms of meditation, dowsing, biodynamic farming, Theosophy, healing, and many other subjects. From this rich soup of information came growth. The pristine environment and fellowship of fertile minds enhanced our spiritual journey.

Patti's book attests to our potential. Her courage is humbling as she shares her remarkable journey. She demonstrates that we use a minute portion of our power; we are an ocean of potentiality.

Today some of the new frontiers we ventured over twenty-five years ago are commonplace. There is a New Age section in every bookshop. Magazines and papers are devoted to the subjects of personal development and spirituality. Recently a documentary, 'Down the Rabbit Hole', brought together scientists and mystics exploring quantum mechanics, neurobiology, and human consciousness.

This book is confronting and evocative, but I believe that in twenty-five years time the experiences Patti has shared will be as acceptable as sprouts and tofu in Coles.

Beverley Collett
26th February 2007

Human Crystals

First Contact

I love the early hours of the morning when most people are fast asleep. The soft quiet of minds at rest gives me space to be.

There was a hint of light on the horizon, allowing me to pick my way through the dew-covered grass to the magnificent karri tree near the centre of our property. I shivered with the freshness of the gentle breeze and drew my cotton blanket snugly around my shoulders. Everything smelt fresh with the scent of the tea tree bushes near the dam, and the earth beneath my bare feet seemed to reach up to greet me. I sat on a log of wood in my favourite position facing the tree, and meditated.

An unusual ice-blue light bathed me as soon as I had completed the cleansing phase of my meditation. I tried to do my usual count 1, 2, 3 into my peaceful scene, the sacred space where I converse with male and female aspects of my higher self; but the blue light was all-encompassing. The image of my peaceful scene was obliterated by the intensity of the beautiful energy field. A disembodied, hazy face appeared in the blue.

"We come in peace, we love you," the face telepathically communicated to me. The light enveloped me physically with a silky smoothness, and the face hovered before me.

I tried to change the appearance of the face with my creative imagination. I wanted it to look more human! A tug of war ensued with my intellect, which was having trouble with the fact that the face had the classic extraterrestrial large dark eyes, no hair, indistinct nose and a slit for a mouth.

"This is nonsense, Patti. You are seeing an ET face because you want to see an ET!" said my logic.

"So how come I can't change the face to something else?" I countered.

I sharply sucked in my breath as I realized that this was no meditation; this was actually happening!

"We come in peace, we love you," the face repeated after my mental arguments subsided into stunned silence. "We ask permission for you to allow the blue energy into your body."

I liked the fact that I had a choice, so I agreed. Opening the crown chakra at the top of my head, I breathed in the soft blue light, allowing it to be drawn through the core of my body and out my feet into the ground. I was bathed in peace and a sense of belonging, yet my body was vibrating with intensity.

My fear of deluding myself with the answers I might receive prevented me from asking the being any questions. I abruptly ended the meditation in a state of perturbation. So many questions buzzed through my head: Why did the being talk in the plural "we"? Was it really an ET, or did it manifest that way to make it easier for me to converse with it/them? Was I going to tell anyone about this? – Hell, no!

Why was this happening now? Well, I figured, I had recently changed the beginning of my meditation significantly.

2

Since learning Alexander Everett's technique way back in 1978, I had developed a routine of focusing on each of the seven main chakras (energy centres) in turn and visualizing the associated colour emanating from each. My intention and the vibration of the colour cleansed and energized each chakra and nourished the related area of the body.

Red is for the base chakra, which is level with the base of the spine. The second chakra is orange, level with the navel and the top of the hips. The solar plexus area is yellow, the heart is green, blue is for the throat, indigo is focused in the third eye area and violet is the crown chakra at the top of the head. Upon entering my imaginary sanctuary, which had a waterfall and stream set in a beautiful pristine forest, I would receive inspiration from my guides. These meditations were visual and metaphorical; like lucid dreaming.

After fourteen years of doing the same meditation I was ready to add a bit of spice to it. The change had occurred two months prior to the contact with the being, when I read in a crystal healing book a beautiful prayer:

> I invoke the Light of the Christ within
> I am a clear and perfect channel
> I am guided by the Light

It occurred to me that, like a crystal, I could cleanse myself with this prayer, so I replaced visualizing the colours of the chakras with this invocation. Silently I would say this prayer three times into each chakra in turn, then go 1, 2, 3 into my peaceful scene as usual to commune with my guides. Sometimes I would replace the prayer with three Oms (pronounced A-U-M). Om is the primal sound and the most sacred word of the Indian Vedas. It is the symbol of God and of Brahman.

3

I guessed that the months of invocation of the prayer and the Oming had attracted a different vibration, intention or reality to me: the blue light beings.

My curiosity was aroused, so later on the same morning of the initial contact, I meditated again. The blue light being was waiting for me.

"We come in peace, we love you. We are a group consciousness; a collective of individual beings functioning as a cohesive whole."

I had the sense that the blue light was the consciousness of the beings, or at least the medium through which they communicated with me.   The beings asked me to swallow a small ethereal scroll, like a photographic film. I put it in my mouth, chewed it and swallowed. Like popcorn bursting to life, my mind exploded with the expansion of the microfilm into a huge library of information. It looked like a photograph of bands of DNA, a long strip of alternating light and dark stripes stretching out to infinity. I was incredulous!

"We have just downloaded you with information that will help you to communicate with us. You will write a book."

"What? I'm not a writer," I protested. "And I don't have anything of value to write about! What is this book about?"

No response. I could feel our minds were still connected, but either they just weren't going to tell me or my mind was refusing to hear the answer.

Man, had they picked the wrong person to write a book for them! The idea of channelling a book was both exciting and abhorrent to me. I knew my rational mind would do battle with the idea of surrendering control enough for the beings' ideas to flow through. Who was I kidding? – I have no writing skills. This must be my big fat Ego holding court, surely!

"You will write a book," they reiterated. "In fact, you will write four books."

I laughed out loud at that one. How ridiculous! I finished this meditation feeling even more perplexed than after the first encounter.

In the next few meditations I was instructed to bring down a red and blue light together, which created a beautiful purple colour. Then they reverted to the blue colour only. To my great relief, the writing of the book(s) was not mentioned again. The energy of the beings was loving, yet curiously detached and neutral. They always honoured me by asking permission before doing anything with me.

*

Three months after my first contact with the beings I drove from my home in Torbay, in the southwest of Western Australia, up to Dwellingup near Perth. I loved coming to Nanga Bush Camp to teach on Supercamp.

The gravel crunched under my tyres, causing dust to enter the vents as I drove up the winding track to the jarrah plank and bush pole cabins nestled in the heart of the dense native forest. A smile played on my lips at the thought of seeing everyone again. A lovely bunch of inspirational people worked on Supercamp. They walked their talk and were passionate about helping kids to excel, communicate more effectively and be happy in their own skin.

Big hugs all round greeted me when I entered the main meeting hall and joyously reconnected with Terrie, Nicole,

Ross, Joel, Belinda and James, who were busy doing final preparations. James enveloped me in his arms, then gently squeezed while rocking me side to side.

"It's great to see you again!" he chuckled in my ear.

"James, it's always a delight to spend time with you," I responded affectionately.

"You're bunking in the youngsters' camp this time, Patti," beamed James. "The teens' camp is full up – eighty-one kids."

"Great! How many are there in the primary school camp?"

"It's full too. There are about sixty-five, but Derry will be able to tell you for sure."

I drove through the bush past the obstacle course and the abseiling tower to the youngsters' camp. This camp was smaller and had a more intimate feel, which was reassuring for any kids prone to homesickness.

"You'll have more peace and quiet down this end," explained Derry as he ushered me into my sleeping quarters. My eyes scanned two bunk beds. Some staff had already arrived and claimed their sleeping spots. I put my gear on a bottom bunk and left with Derry to meet the volunteer support staff.

Derry was the perfect choice for the youngsters' camp coordinator. Little kids warm to him as he is a wonderful mixture of playful kid, loving father figure and disciplined teacher.

The instructors and support staff lined up outside to greet the busloads of children. I positioned myself so that I could observe the children as they alighted. I made a mental note of who was looking upset or hesitant so that I could give them a helping hand and check how they were faring as the days progressed. I had already scanned the medical records and identified which kids were on medication, which had learning and/or behavioural problems. These were the kids that I might be giving private sessions of Brain Gym balances to.

My primary role on camp was as an Educational Kinesiologist, or Brain Gym instructor as it is more generically known. Brain Gym® was developed by Dr Paul E. Dennison and his wife Gail as a purely educational model, independent of any philosophy. It is a movement-based, highly effective system of targeted activities that prepares the brain and entire nervous system for optimal performance in all areas, intellectual, creative, athletic and interpersonal.

The teens' and youngsters' camps ran simultaneously but independently of each other, with only a couple of staff, including me, teaching at both camps. The whole property was continually abuzz with rotating activities such as white water rafting, abseiling, team building, study skills, Neuro Linguistic Programming, Brain Gym, juggling, songs, trust games, storytelling, archery, playback theatre and crafts.

Each morning I taught twenty minutes of Brain Gym movements to lively music with positive lyrics. I stood on a platform so that the youngsters and staff could easily follow me, and invited half a dozen kids onto the stage to demonstrate with me. Afterwards, I jogged three hundred meters through the bush to the Teens Camp and enjoyed twenty minutes of Brain Gym to music with the teenagers.

I had different sessions throughout each day, in both camps. With twenty-five kids at a time, I taught various Brain Gym

Action balances to improve writing and spelling, reading and hand/eye coordination, listening and memory skills. One of the more transformational sessions I led was a Repatterning process integrating the three dimensions of the brain and body for the group goal: *I love, value and respect myself.*

Assisting in trust games, communication skills and playback theatre was a real buzz for me. I particularly enjoyed acting out the highlights and antics that the children experienced during their week on camp. They loved the staff doing playbacks of their stories.

*

Once again it was time for me to share the rag doll stretch with the teenagers. This was always done on a night towards the end of the camp so that everyone was used to each other. The lights were dimmed and soothing music was played continually. The session was experienced en masse, eighty-five teens with a few supervisors spaced around the room to caution anyone being too rough.

Everyone chose a partner they felt comfortable with. Mattresses were placed on the floor and one person lay down fully clothed and relaxed while their partner slowly and gently moved each joint of the fingers, then the wrist, elbow, shoulder and whole arm in turn. The entire body was systematically manipulated and massaged, while the person receiving lay as limp and floppy as a rag doll.

The intention of the session was to learn to be fully present with your partner, giving them your undivided attention in a respectful and unconditionally loving manner, then to swap over and allow yourself to trust, relax and receive fully. Initially there were always a few nervous giggles and the odd ill-at-ease person horse-playing. When given the option of sitting out and watching, they always chose to continue with the stretch, promising to calm down and be gentler. They really didn't want to miss out!

Gradually the boisterous lads discovered it was okay and actually pleasurable (heaven forbid) to be gentle with each other. By the time they came to swap over everyone had settled. The session concluded with the room exuding harmony and stillness.

After the session, Belinda and I headed towards the swimming hole, leaving the night staff to settle the kids in their bunks and patrol for mischievous pranksters. There was adequate moonlight to find our way along the path without our torches, but occasionally we would grab each other to steady ourselves as we slipped and skated on the gum nuts beneath our feet.

We sat quiescent, drinking in the stillness after a jam-packed day. Eventually we broke the silence by sharing significant events in our lives since the last camp. I knew Belinda had an interest in spirituality, metaphysics and ETs, so I broached the subject uppermost in my mind.

"Have you ever had contact with ETs?"

"I've had some amazing meditations and experiences but not physical contact," replied Belinda. "Have you?"

"No. . . . Well to tell the truth, I'm not sure. I've been conversing in my meditations with these beings that have a group consciousness. At first I thought I was deluding myself, but strange things have been happening at night lately."

"Like what?"

"I see vague shapes and movement in the bedroom as I'm drifting off to sleep. I feel spooked and panic, then the next

9

thing I know, it's morning! Sometimes I wake up in the middle of the night feeling myself being moved sideways and lifted off the bed."

"Wow! What's it like?" I had Belinda's full attention.

"It's the same sensation as when I've had an anaesthetic in hospital and been moved from the operating table to the bed. I'm vaguely aware that someone is moving me but I have no control of the situation and quickly lapse into unconsciousness."

Belinda waited for me to continue.

"Whenever I lie down, my whole body starts vibrating and buzzing with energy. It goes on for up to twenty minutes."

"Hey, that's been happening to me too!" enthused Belinda. "I think the universal energy is accelerating right now. Many authors talk about the physical phenomena we will experience as the consciousness of humanity shifts into the forth and fifth dimensional reality. You'd love Norma Milanovich's book, *We the Arcturians*," she added. "It's about these group consciousness beings that she communicates with from the star system Arcturus. They telepathically transmit information to her. At the moment I'm reading a very amusing book called *ET 101*. It's tongue-in-cheek yet hits the spot about the channelling, ET and Walk In phenomena."

"Who's the author?"

"Don't know off-hand. Let's go back to camp and I'll show it to you."

In Belinda's room I noted down the titles and authors of both books. *ET 101* by Dianna Luppi and Mission Control looked like an easy read. I resolved to purchase both books Belinda had told me about in the hope that they would shed some light on what was happening to me.

*

In late autumn that year, three friends who had attended a Denise Lynn workshop came to our property to do a vision quest. The beaches and state forests near my place were perfect for it. Unfortunately the vision quest proved quite challenging for the women. The weather turned sour and they had to endure hours and hours of exposure to driving rain and winds. By the time I picked them up from their respective nature retreats they were drenched and bordering on hypothermic.

During this visit my friend Susie and I drove to Albany to stock up on yummy food. Driving home in the early evening we spotted a pulsating green light in the sky. It moved straight up in the air then did a sharp 90-degree turn left and vanished, leaving a green trail for a moment. Susie slammed on the brakes and pulled over.

"Did you see that!" she squawked.

"Yeah!" I said in amazement.

The whole sighting had only taken a couple of minutes – possibly even less than that. If we hadn't both seen it I might have dismissed it as imagination. Neither of us said a word to anyone else when we returned home, as if we had an unspoken pact of secrecy. This was the first sighting of a possible UFO I had ever experienced. I wondered if it had any connection to my blue light friends.

The Lessons Begin

In 1993 I decided to move back to Perth with the two most important people in my life, my twin teenage sons, Adam and Craig. My niece Katie and her boyfriend Paul shared a house with us in Fremantle. I worked full time at my WA Kinesiology Centre and the boys settled into their new high school.

I was still receiving guidance from the blue light beings which I now called my guides. Feeling a palpable presence in the room at night became so commonplace I used to say out loud, "Hi guys!" then go to sleep and let them get to work. My initial anxiety had given way to familiarity. I had no idea what went on at night, but I wasn't worried as no harm appeared to be being done to me. I knew that psychic abilities were definitely being activated in me during the nocturnal visits. My clairaudient skills had developed to the point that my guides could get my attention and chat telepathically to me even while I was doing housework.

One night in November that year as I went to sleep, I asked my guides out loud for some physical proof of their presence as I felt I needed a reality check. There was a thunderstorm that night, and unusually cool, so I threw an extra blanket on the bed. I hunkered down, had a particularly sound sleep and woke up feeling like something had been resolved in my dreams.

The next morning Katie popped her head around my bedroom door and inquired, "Did you sleep all right?"

"Yeah, great!" I replied. "Why? What's up?" – reading the curious expression on her face. She sat wide-eyed on the bed and told me the story.

"In the middle of the night Paul and I were woken up by a large orange glowing ball of light hovering in the air right inside our bedroom!"

"No kidding?"

Katie shook her head. "It was intensely hot and there was a high-pitched ringing/humming sound. The sound would get louder and louder, then suddenly turn down in pitch and volume, only to crank up again." She looked at me with her eyebrows raised, waiting for my response. I looked blankly back at her. "We were dripping wet with the intensity of the heat coming off the thing," she continued. "And we sat clutching each other in terror, not daring to take our eyes off it."

"How long did it last?"

"Three hours. The longest three hours of my life! Then it just vanished as suddenly as it had come. Poof!"

I was incredulous, so I went into their bedroom and quizzed Paul, expecting him to offer a logical explanation. He repeated Katie's story and confessed he was scared shitless!

"Could the wind or the street light have created that effect?" I asked.

"Definitely not," was his reply. "The light and the sound were physically in the room. It was so hot we were drenched in sweat."

"Did you look outside?"

"You're kidding, right? There was no way I was going anywhere!"

"What do you think caused it?"

He hesitated and then said, "I haven't got a clue; it was out of the realm of anything I know."

It was wise of my guides to give me confirmation of their presence through a dramatic display for Katie and Paul so that I couldn't dismiss it.

*

That summer *The Book of Knowledge: The Keys of Enoch* by J.J. Hurtak arrived in the mail from the USA. My Texan friend, Wynelle, dowsed using her pendulum that I should have it; so she sent it to me as a present.

In the early 1980s, when Wynelle was living in Perth, she taught me creative visualization incorporating the therapeutic use of dance and the expressive arts as a personal development tool. Her original training was in nursing with a specialization in paediatrics. Her work as a dance/movement therapist in psychiatric settings with adults led to using these skills in stress management and personal growth with adults. She also introduced me to Jack Johnston's doctoral research on dream interpretation of the Senoi, a mountain tribe on the island of Timor. The Senoi practise dream analysis on a daily basis, with their families, to assist with personal and community problem solving. Wynelle taught me how to have a dialogue with characters from my dreams to gain information from my subconscious.

Over the years Wynelle has been a major inspiration and teacher for me, generously sharing her knowledge and experience. She has worked extensively with Jean Houston, Dr Brugh Joy and esoteric philosopher/educator William David. Now she is passionately involved with radionics, vibrational healing of the subtle energy fields, dowsing and noetic sciences.

When I received *The Keys of Enoch* it was not available in Perth's esoteric bookstores, yet the first publishing and copyright was 1973. The inside cover read:

> *A Teaching Given On Seven Levels*
> *To be Read and Visualized*
> *In Preparation for the Brotherhood of Light*
> *To be Delivered for the Quickening of the*
> *"People of Light"*

A large chunk of the book was incomprehensible and overwhelming in its concepts, but I ploughed through it anyway. I trusted that it was triggering something on other levels and that its significance would become apparent later. The Great White Brotherhood, the Ascended Masters and the Christ Consciousness featured throughout the book.

The Great White Brotherhood, also known as the Brotherhood of The All, is a confederation of Ascended Masters. It also includes members of the Heavenly Host, a spiritual hierarchy directly concerned with the evolution of humanity and Earth. The name, Brotherhood, does not imply any gender or racial discrimination, and includes males, females and androgenous beings. "White" refers to the aura, or halo, of white light surrounding these beings, indicating a high vibrational frequency and level of spiritual evolvement. Ascended Masters are holy people who have reached a high degree of spirituality, left the Earth plane and ascended into higher dimensions. Examples of those believed to be Ascended Masters are Jesus, Confucius, Gautama Buddha, Mary the mother of Jesus, Lord Maitreya, Saint Germain and Master Kuthumi.

To my surprise Archturus (as it was spelt in *The Keys of Enoch*) had a whole section devoted to it. It was described as a midway station providing knowledge on all levels to educate planetary intelligence. I remembered reading in Norma Milanovich's book all the amazing details that the Arcturians had communicated to her. Also Lyssa Royal in *The Prism of Lyra* describes Arcturus as an archetype or future-self ideal of Earth and that the Arcturians assist humans in healing personal and planetary consciousness. Lyssa also comments that they are primarily a sixth density vibration which has been attributed to the angelic kingdom.

Several months later Wynelle dowsed that I should also be the caretaker of a Galactic Wand. When it arrived in the mail I was struck with awe by the nine-inch quartz crystal with a terminal at each end. It was so brilliantly clear it looked like glass, and down each side were hundreds of little facets. This was a laboratory-grown, cultured crystal made of very pure silica dioxide. When it was held to the light, a faint straight line could be seen where it had been grown on a string.

The crystal sent to me was one of two hundred complete wands and fifty shards found in Arkansas, USA. Wynelle had custodianship of twenty-two wands and seven shards. Each wand had a different number and type of notches down the sides. Only two wands had no notches at all.

Several psychics had tuned into these crystals and came up with some intriguing information. They reported that each wand contained hundreds of programs. The actual content of these programs was not available to be interpreted literally. What was most surprising was *the wands did not need cleansing, the programs could not be tampered with and no new programs could be added.*

The Galactic Wands were impressive because Wynelle couldn't erase, add to, or alter the existing programs in them. The existing programs remained permanently. By contrast, all naturally grown quartz crystals need regular cleansing and the programs can be changed as the need arises. Wynelle regularly puts healing programs into naturally grown quartz crystals as part of her work, using a traditional radionics box that energises through magnetism, or by using two-dimensional mandalas, or combinations of sacred geometric shapes. An ordinary quartz crystal can be cleared by holding the tip and bottom of the crystal, then squeezing the ends while blowing on the crystal. This alters the piezoelectric arrangement both on and within the crystal, and automatically clears the programs within the crystal.

To cleanse a crystal of non-beneficial energy distortions, place it in sea salt (or rock salt) for at least 20 hours. Alternatively, you can cleanse a crystal under fresh, running cold water, or by placing it in sunlight for a period of time. Experienced energy workers can cleanse crystals by running energy through their hands into the crystal while holding clear and focused thoughts toward cleansing the crystal.

Wynelle met with a psychic friend three times to find out more about the Galactic Wands. Some of the information gleaned from the crystals is as follows:

The Galactic Wands have group energy, which is rare. Whoever has a wand, or a group of them, will be attuned to all the crystals. The crystals were created by extraterrestrial and human collaboration. This was the fifth attempt through the ages by the extraterrestrials to use the crystals to create a harmonious and peaceful network of communication with humanity on a world-wide basis. There seemed to be a strong intention towards collective thought harmonics.

The two Wands with no notches down the sides were to be planted in good quality planting soil for three months. They were to act as antennae to serve as a connecting communication link to other crystals planted around the planet.

The purpose of the Wands seemed to be to abate planetary turmoil, pressures and worries, and to bring forward and oppose anything that is in the way of the Light of the person possessing them. This implied that "unfinished business" in the person would be shaken loose, dealt with and cleared. The Wands are of the Light, and when they touch darkness, they stir change in it.

Wynelle was told that the man who found the crystals originally was almost sent mad by the force of their energies. Apparently if you are not prepared to look at and release your negativity, blocks or limitations, the crystals will amplify and reflect these back, making it hard to live with yourself. This man passed on the wands like hot potatoes. They eventually found their way to a psychic woman who understood their value and origins. She in turn asked Wynelle to be guardian of some of them.

*

I felt honoured that this crystal had come into my life. I meditated with it each day and put it by my head while I slept. Initially I had to adjust to the high vibration of the

Wand. Waves of energy, heat and light would move through me when I held it, causing hot flushes and dizziness. This was an extraordinary crystal!

From the time the wand came into my life everything accelerated. Lessons came thick and fast. I was in the habit of clearing issues for myself with Kinesiology balances, past life regressions, flower essences and/or meditation. The number of balances I did for myself had to increase dramatically in order to keep pace with the changes.

Kinesiology uses muscle monitoring to measure stress and imbalance in the body, emotions, mind and spirit. There are many techniques available in Kinesiology to bring the whole system into better postural alignment and health. It is also useful for personal development and transformation. Sometimes we may be painfully aware of our shortcomings and irrational reactivity to people or situations, but feel doomed to repeat the same pattern like a stuck record. At other times we are ignorant of how our behaviour and unconscious belief systems are affecting our perspective on reality and those around us. Using the tools of Kinesiology, I am able to observe myself more clearly and I am free to choose a better way of being; it puts me back in the driver's seat, so to speak.

*

When I travelled overseas, the Galactic Wand went with me. While I was visiting a friend in France the crystal was accidentally dropped, smashing into three roughly equal pieces and a tiny triangular chip. Initially I was horrified, and my friend Jean-Luc, who had dropped it, was mortified! Later that day I meditated and tuned into the crystal pieces. The message I received surprised me. The crystal was meant to be broken! The programs were not distorted or lost and the pieces were operating as if they were intact. I naturally wondered if the message was wishful thinking on my part.

Two months later when I was back in Perth, Wynelle arrived from the USA for a visit. I guiltily showed her the broken wand. She dowsed over the crystal pieces.

"Don't worry, Patti. The crystal seems to have deliberately broken itself," consoled Wynelle. "It's as if it has a consciousness of its own. The programs are not lost or distorted in any way!"

My relief was immense. I had not told Wynelle prior to her dowsing what I had received in meditation on the day that it was dropped. The psychics must have been right when they said the programs couldn't be altered.

The Dreamtime Calls

I continued to meditate twice daily and sometimes more often than that.

"We come in peace and we love you." The loving, soothing pale blue energy was here again. "We want you to breathe down the blue energy from the tenth level." I had no idea what the tenth level was, so I brought down the energy from my tenth chakra high above my head. I created a beautiful column of light and drew down the energy 10, 9, 8, 7 (crown of head), 6 (third eye) ....down to the base chakra (tailbone).

"Now draw the energy down through your feet and connect with the earth." A sense of peace, love and belonging filled my whole being as I did this.

"Make the cylinder of light as wide as the room." I expanded the energy field. "Good. Now make it as big as the whole house and yard. Hold it there."

These mental gymnastics were hard to do. Initially I couldn't maintain the column the same width all the way down. At certain chakra levels the energy field would dent or collapse and I had to really focus to push it back out again.

From then on I always included the 8th, 9th and 10th chakras, located in my aura above my head, when I affirmed three times into each chakra my usual prayer:

> *I invoke the Light of the Christ within*
> *I am a clear and perfect channel*
> *I am guided by the Light.*

This exercise became a daily practice. Once I had mastered it I would bring down the column of light while driving. I was instructed to hold the energy, as wide as the road, until I had passed ten traffic lights. This was one of several exercises my guides would ask me to do. I didn't know what all this was for, but it was a lot of fun and good for my concentration.

*

In August 1994 Jean-Luc stayed with me for two weeks at the tail end of a business trip. During the time he visited, I spent more time socializing with Aborigines than I had in my whole life previously. They recognize this outgoing Frenchman as a brother no matter where in Australia he goes.

One night I woke up to the sound of didgeridoos playing in my head. Looking up I saw four bearded, longhaired Aboriginal spirit men walk through the wall and across to my bed. Each man had a long spear in his left hand. I was stunned. My eyes were open, I was awake and I was hearing didgeridoos playing and seeing ghosts!

This was a first for me. I was more fascinated than frightened. I closed my eyes but I could still see them. I opened my eyes again and saw a male Aboriginal face clear as day, four centimetres away from mine. This time I jumped! Talk about being in your face! I didn't know what they wanted as there was no dialogue. Eventually I fell asleep again.

A few days after this, Jean-Luc and I went to a weekend gathering of indigenous Australians which Auntie was conducting with her friends. Again, this time in broad daylight, I saw the same four spirit men walk across the lawn to Jean-Luc. From then on my ability to see Aboriginal spirits was firmly established. I had no idea why this ability had suddenly manifested.

*

Penny, Maggie, Auntie, Diane and I were having a meeting in Maggie's kitchen to discuss the idea of creating an Australian version of the Canadian Rediscovery camps. Indian elders taught children about tribal law and customs, natural sciences and survival skills while camping in wilderness areas. We thought that something similar would be great for Australian kids to connect with the land, learn some bush lore and find out about the Dreamtime.

Maggie's door is always open to her friends and we often congregated in her home. She is a generous-hearted, loyal, "salt of the earth" woman with an ample bosom to hug you to. Don't let her 148cm height fool you, though. Maggie is an ex-state champion hockey goalie; not much gets past her. Her startling clear blue eyes see everything.

Quietly smiling and drawing on her cigarette was Auntie. Her mob (tribe) comes from the Central Desert. As an elder and keeper of the law, Auntie has contact with Aborigines from all over Australia. Auntie spends so much time conversing with the spirit world, the Dreamtime; it is sometimes hard to keep up with the drift of her conversation.

23

While we white women nattered about the logistics of running camps for kids with Aboriginal elders, Auntie sat and listened. Occasionally she would add a message from spirit. The air in the room changed and I felt an energetic shift as Auntie worked on what we called *the inside way*. She is a great example of how to appear to be doing nothing while changing everything.

Working in this manner is similar to changing channels on the television; you switch to another frequency or band of vibration. You can quickly send messages to other people across great expanses; time and distance are not a limitation. On this other channel Auntie can converse with the Dreamtime, retrieve information and do healing of the Earth and its people via the Song Lines. The Song Lines are called Ley Lines in Europe and Dragon Lines in China. They are channels of energy like the Earth's acupuncture meridians.

Doing work on *the inside way* is like being in two places simultaneously. When I see my guides/angels or Aboriginal spirits, it is rather like a photograph that has a double exposure: overlapping the "real" world is another reality. Two worlds/dimensions coexist in the same place; one is just a little clearer and more solid than the other. These beings are visible to the eye but are not solid. I see them with my eyes open while being able to see through them. They are of a higher/faster vibration than our physical world. My dreams overlap my meditations, which overlap my waking reality. They are continuous and connected.

We had a wonderful, stimulating and enthusiastic morning together. The magnitude of the project and the tribal, cultural issues to be overcome were daunting. Everyone had unique knowledge and experience to contribute to the project. Maggie had worked closely with Auntie for years. Penny was actively involved in the Greens Party and was well informed on land rights, the Heritage Act, and so on. She had recently been to Canada visiting reservations and talking with native American chiefs, comparing the problems and progress of their indigenous communities to those of the Australian Aborigines. Diane had just completed a degree in Anthropology, majoring in Aboriginal studies.

It would be easy for me to transfer the skills I shared on Supercamp; however, it was the Aboriginal side of things that I needed experience with. I admitted that I had almost no knowledge of Aboriginal law or the Dreamtime. I stated that my first priority was to do something about this lack. The meeting concluded with nothing concrete being organised; or so I thought!

At one o'clock that night, Maggie called me in great distress. "Patti, sorry to disturb you but I'm freaking out!"

"God, what's wrong? What happened?" I was very concerned because Maggie is usually level-headed and unshakable. She had never rung me in desperation about anything before.

"Something energetic is happening that I can't quite put my finger on." From the tone of her voice I could tell that something had really spooked Maggie.

"Hang on honey; I'm coming over to your place now."

I woke Katie and explained that I was going to Maggie's so she, Craig and Adam wouldn't be worried in the morning. When I arrived Maggie was apologetic. "I'm so sorry to drag you out in the middle of the night." Everything felt okay to me in the house but she was very agitated. Maggie's husband John and her three teenage boys were all fast asleep.

So as to not disturb John, we slept on mattresses on the floor in her Reiki healing room. Several times during the remainder of the night I was woken by the sound of clapping sticks and a line of Aboriginal spirit women singing and dancing before me. The women were holding their elbows and moving their arms side to side as if rocking a baby as they shuffled their feet in unison. It was a very joyful experience.

I shared the night's events with Maggie the next morning. We decided that the nocturnal visitations were caused by sleeping beneath her Aboriginal initiation law stick.

Later that morning I was surprised to receive a phone call at Maggie's place from Mary, a woman I had met only a few times before. She had tracked me down to ask if I wanted to go to the Kimberley area of northwest Australia to spend a week camping out in the bush with an Aboriginal elder, learning about the Dreamtime! I laughed and laughed, incredulous that my prayers had been answered, literally overnight. I knew in my heart that Auntie had helped to create this.

A few days later Diane, Penny, Maggie, a photographer and talented artist named Jan and I met with Mary at her place to discuss the details of the trip up north. The plan was for Mary and four others to fly to Derby, pick up David Mowaljarlai, and four-wheel-drive inland through his tribal land. We would sleep in the bush under the stars in swags every night. During the day David would tell us Dreamtime stories, teaching us about the landscape and his people, the Ngarinyin. I knew there would be much that David would not be able to share with us because of tribal law but I was keen to learn whatever he chose to share with us. Mary told us Mowal, as she affectionately called him, was Aboriginal of the Year 1991 and was made a Member of The Order of Australia in 1993.

Penny decided she couldn't go. Maggie and Diane were unsure. I had never been surer about anything in my life. I told the group that irrespective of whether they were coming or not, I knew I had to go! I intuitively knew that this trip was vital for me and would be somehow personally transformational. Maggie wanted to go but finances were tight. I paid Maggie in advance for a Second Degree Reiki course I wanted to attend and Maggie was set. Diane decided she would go too; so the final grouping was Mary, Jan, Maggie, Diane and me.

Preparation

From the time I moved back to Perth in 1993, the blue light beings instructed me to journal all my significant experiences, dreams and meditations. Right up to the present I have continued this practice.

My guides told me I needed to prepare for the trip up north and gave me a list of things to do each day:

- Sing the Gayatri Mantra, the universal prayer:

    Om bhur bhuva sva; tat savitur varenyam
    Bhargo devasya deemahi;
    Dheeyoyona prachodayat
    Om shanti; shanti; shanti

    We meditate on that Supreme Effulgence of
    the Radiant Being,
    The indwelling controller and director of all
    things.
    May he stimulate our intellect entirely (to
    realize the truth).
    Om peace; peace; peace

My favourite translation is from *The New Book of Runes* by Ralph Blum:

> *You who are the source of all power,*
> *Whose rays illuminate the whole world,*
> *Illuminate also my heart*
> *So that it too can do your work*

- <u>Do toning.</u> This entails making spontaneous soundings or tones which produce specific resonances that activate the chakras. The Tibetan Buddhists are experts at toning and create beautiful harmonics or overtones.

- <u>Place Bach Flower Essences on my calves and heart chakra</u>. I thought that this was an unusual request and I was unclear why the essences needed to be on those specific areas. Flower essences are a form of vibrational healing which stimulates change physically, mentally, emotionally and spiritually.

- <u>Hug a tree to ground myself</u>. I love trees so this activity was a delight for me. I had worked part-time teaching Reforestation and Whole Farm Planning in Torbay and for many years did volunteer winter tree planting with my sons.

- <u>Seven times do the Salute to the Sun</u>. This sequence of yoga moves is wonderful for limbering and toning the body.

- For the next task I received an image of me panting. I asked Maggie what panting would have to do with balancing my energies. She immediately related it to <u>Osho's Chakra Meditation</u> and lent me her copy of it. Osho is another name for Bagwan Shree

Rajneesh. His followers were locally called the Orange People because of their orange coloured garb.

This is a forty-five minute meditation where you breathe heavily through your mouth as you focus on each chakra in turn, from the base chakra up to the crown and back down again. This breathing technique sounds like panting. You move your focus and breathing up and down the seven main chakras three times in the forty-five minutes. It is done standing with the feet hip width apart, knees, hips and arms relaxed as you rhythmically bounce up and down to music. This was what I did twice a day until we went on the trip.

- Whirling dervish dancing. Yes, I had heard of this Sufi meditation technique, but where the hell was I going to find out how to do it properly in Perth? I asked around and to my surprise and delight discovered there was a group meeting in my suburb, just ten minutes' drive from my home!

I thought that because of my professional ballet background, I would find twirling on the spot as if one foot was nailed to the floor for forty-five minutes relatively easy. Wrong! In the first session I found myself twice having to lie down on the floor with my whole world spinning, feeling green as grass and doing everything I could to prevent my lunch from going on public display.

One of the main reasons for doing the whirling is to draw higher vibration energies down to the Earth.

- Smoke a peace pipe. This one was going to be tricky. I knew Mary had done a lot of drumming workshops, sweat lodges and vision quests so I asked her if she had one. She did indeed have a peace pipe but she felt that she could not do justice to the sacredness of the ceremony. I thought, "Oh well, that's one thing from my list I won't be able to do."

- <u>Embrace the lizard energy</u> by lying in the sun on a hot rock when up in the Kimberly region.

As usual I was only given information on "a need to know" basis. I didn't have a clue why this unusual combination of techniques was required. As they would not harm me and would probably benefit me, I did them.

*

Lizards and birds are my messengers. They get my attention and telepathically communicate messages to me when Spirit wants me to do things.

When I was living in Torbay, a huge eagle used to regularly ride the thermals in lazy spirals over our property. The eagle was my main animal messenger in meditations.

Many years ago in meditation, the eagle metaphorically represented me. I started out as a vulnerable, scruffy and weak eaglet strengthened by an enormous parent eagle. Over many months of meditations, the parent eagle taught me to grow strong and fly. Eventually I grew to the same size and strength as my parent. I was given exercises to do, such as flying from one mountaintop to another or overcoming obstacles, fear and doubt. I was taught to see with the eyes of an eagle, truthful, clear and sharp.

This and all the seemingly unrelated meditation and spiritual gymnastics requested by my guides, was training me for a future task that I was unaware of. Without this background, what I am going to tell you next won't make sense.

A few days before we flew to Derby to meet with David, I had a powerful meditation: I was instructed to become an eagle again, only this time I had to make myself as big as a mountain. Once this was accomplished I flew to a sacred mountain and landed on top of it. It was no effort to fly, despite being that enormous. My guides asked me to become one with the mountain, so I merged my eagle body with the land and my form turned crystalline. Sometimes I have meditations that literally change the reality of my everyday life. This was one of them. I knew in my bones that I had agreed to do something significant, but I didn't know consciously what it was. Symbolically, something had already been accomplished on the inner levels, and would be followed through and manifested in the physical world.

Wandjina Dreaming

Finally, after much excited preparation, the big day came. Instinctively I had packed two of the crystal pieces. I could feel, with an intense certainty, the importance of this trip, although I was completely in the dark as to why or how it was so. Yes, I was going to learn about the Dreamtime, but the pull to go was more profound than that reason alone accounted for.

It was hard to believe that only one week earlier we had all met at Maggie's to discuss kids' camps with Aboriginal elders. How magical and fast-paced my life was becoming.

As the plane took off I could hear and see the line of dancing Aboriginal spirit women whom I had seen in Maggie's healing room. The women were singing me home! With this realization my heart opened and my eyes filled with tears of joy. The Dreaming of the Kimberly people is the Wandjina, the sky people – maybe this was my connection. The Wandjina, in paintings that Mary had shown me, are similar in appearance to the blue light beings that first contacted me.

In Derby we picked up the four wheel drive, bought provisions and went to meet David. He was tall, slim and very dark skinned, with an air of quiet dignity. David had a peculiarly innocent, boyish smile for a man in his late sixties, and beautiful large, gentle hands. I wondered how he would cope being crammed into the car with five noisy, extroverted white women.

The trip was a wonderful mixture of sacred reverence, as David shared his stories, and joyful play. We headed east and camped the first night at Manning Gorge, a popular tourist spot. That night the sunset was a blaze of orange and red, matching the stunning ochre of the earth.

As I went to sleep I felt an energetic presence move across the camp towards me. I dismissed it as my imagination and rolled over in my swag. That night I had a dream of having my power and integrity challenged. I was pushed and pushed until I was forced to stand my ground and show the full force of my power. The next morning I shared my dream with Maggie and Diane. Maggie said she also felt a presence as she went to sleep and had a dream about Aboriginal women.

After breakfast, David showed us a special place for women near where we had slept. This restful, tree-lined waterhole was where widowed women would live in solitude for a time after the death of their husbands. It was soothing and shady with plenty of fresh water to drink and swim in. It was a beautiful place to mourn. Family members, usually a son, would bring food and leave it for the widow without speaking to her. I saw this as a sign of respect, not as punishment.

I discussed what David had said with Jan. She disagreed with my interpretation. "Patti, I think you have an overly romantic view of things. In reality, being deserted like that for an extended period of time would have been much harsher than you realize."

We broke camp and headed further inland. David made the land come alive for me. Every tree and rocky outcrop held significance and was part of a Dreamtime story. "That ridge over there is a lizard." said David. He went on to tell its

Aboriginal name and the lizard's story. My heart contracted and was saddened when I noticed that the lizard's tail was being mined. Only the stump of a tail was left.

David explained that the Dreamtime stories were and still are his people's school. They teach the children where to find food and good water, which areas are taboo and where there is bad energy. The history of his people, their relationships with neighbouring tribes and social laws, are all laid out in these stories. Each person has a tribal and family totem giving a strong sense of belonging and identity.

At puberty a child becomes an adult and is initiated into the Law. At this time each one is entrusted with certain songs, stories and secrets. As this person matures and is deemed ready, further initiations are undergone. It is a university, the University of Life, where more information and responsibility is given as the person grows in wisdom and experience. Earth is the mother, provider and teacher.

Even though every day the temperature was around thirty-four degrees centigrade, I went barefoot for most of the trip; I didn't want to lose contact with the earth. The Kimberley country is extremely beautiful and singing with life. This place, in my opinion, could reconnect and ground even the most disconnected soul on Earth.

We camped at another waterhole the second night. Each night we lit a fire to cook our food on. David always slept a respectful distance away from us. Jan also liked her space, so she slept alone. This made the camp fairly spread out, with the rowdy ones, Diane, Mary, Maggie and I, sleeping side by side. It was magic to sleep under the vibrant stars where no pollution or town lights obscured the view. Tents weren't necessary, as it was very still and hot. The canvas of our swags kept the dew off.

It was a fabulous feeling being in the outback knowing we were the only people for hundreds of miles. I hadn't felt this joyful and carefree in years. We women swam naked, laughing and frolicking like children. David always respected our space and privacy by occupying himself a hundred yards or so through the bush away from us.

One morning David took us to a sacred site. He stopped in the bush and pointed to some insignificant-looking rocks, which showed to the trained eye where the boundary to the sacred site was. He spoke out loud in his native tongue to the spirits of the site for permission to bring us into the area.

As we stepped over the boundary a wind came up from nowhere, blew eerily for thirty seconds, and then stopped as abruptly as it had started. It had been such a still, hot morning that the significance of the wind seemed obvious. This was his spirit ancestors granting permission. Maggie and I gave each other knowing looks with raised eyebrows.

Every time we entered and left a sacred site, the same wind would usher us in and out. David always asked permission to enter and gave respectful thanks as we left.

On this first site was an enormous four-and-a-half meter, round rock which represented the clouds and rain-making capacity of the Wandjina. To me it looked like a space ship. Next to it were the men's and women's caves covered in ancient paintings of the Wandjina and the sweet water turtle.

The Wandjina looked like extraterrestrials to me, with overly large dark eyes, no mouth or ears and markings around the head like an aura. David explained that the vertical line between the eyes was not a nose. It represented spirit descending into matter. The Wandjina were depicted with heads and shoulders, but no body.

The men's cave looked cared for as it had been relatively recently repainted, giving life and definition to the figures. The woman's cave looked faded and neglected, creating a sense of ebbing energy. He explained that this was for two reasons. Firstly, his people were waiting for an anthropologist to analyse paint samples to date the paintings. Paint had peeled off in many places, exposing several layers of different generations of artists. This would make it easier and more accurate to date them. Second, most of the female elders had died, and with each wet season they were losing more. Fewer and fewer young women were interested in going through the law, so there was no-one to paint the caves. This depletion of power and focus was tangible in the paintings.

David collected rounded leaves from a special tree, made a small fire in the mouth of the men's cave and put the leaves on it. This created a lot of smoke and was done to respect David's ancestors. Suddenly I realized that this was the Aboriginal equivalent of the American Indian peace pipe ceremony! I pulled Maggie to one side and quietly explained what I felt, and she agreed. I asked David if we could please smoke the women's cave also, as I wanted to send power to and honour the women.

As he prepared a fire in the opening of the women's cave, Maggie rolled me a cigarette from her pouch of tobacco. I have never smoked cigarettes, but I wanted to connect in my own way with the ceremony without interfering with it. As David smoked the cave and sang to his ancestors I inhaled deeply on the cigarette, held it in my lungs then blew the smoke towards the paintings and the fire so that our two cultures could mix.

We were then shown a ceremony that mothers and daughters share in. This involves standing on either side of the fire with the mother and daughter facing each other. They then hold right hands together and step across the fire, trading places twice. As I shared this ritual with Diane we were both moved to tears.

All five women present had the greatest respect and reverence for what David was sharing with us. Each one of us was touched by the ceremonies in our own private way. I had smoked my "peace pipe" as per my pre-trip preparatory list from my guides. I wondered where the rock might be to carry out the final instruction, connecting with the lizard energy. As I was thinking this, Jan pointed out a lizard basking in the sun on a flat rock in front of both caves. It was an encouraging sign but I knew that this was not the time or place to do it.

As we left the sacred site David called out thanks to his ancestors on our behalf. The wind came up and ended abruptly as a reply.

At Kennedy River, David showed us a burial site with Wandjina and crocodile paintings. There was a rock shaped unmistakably like a large crocodile head. He brought young boys here to learn Mandangnari Crocodile Dreaming and how to do rock paintings. The Crocodile Rock site was where the long-necked tortoise escaped the men's trap. Each story David told seemed to connect us to the next place we would visit. Gradually he was painting an interconnected picture of the whole landscape through the stories of each place we explored.

David and the boys had been experimenting with modern techniques of application. Aquadhere was used to stick new paint to the old layers. The youngsters didn't know how to mix it in the right proportions with the pigment and it had run in places. To make natural glue for the paint, bark was taken from the Munggundu tree and pulped with stones to extract gum. It was mixed with water to make a sticky red paste. From what I could see, the traditional way had better results.

Around the campfire that night, David talked about Aboriginal healers and their ability to draw out sickness and bad energy through the intact skin of sick people. "When I was a boy, I choked on some food stuck in my throat," David explained. "The medicine man put his mouth over my throat and sucked it right out through my skin, leaving no mark. Another time I was real sick and he drew out bad blood from my stomach and spat it out. The next morning I was better." His description was similar to what I had personally seen Philippine spiritual/psychic healers do. The blood came out with no incision or wound being created.

One time, a child was taken by a crocodile. The men used their power and singing to draw the crocodiles out of the water and kill them. The next morning five crocodiles were found lined up on the riverbank dead. There was one croc lying higher up the bank than the others – The men's power had drawn that one up further. This higher crocodile was cut open and inside were the bones of the young boy. The men were able to take the bones for a proper burial.

In the Kimberley region the indigenous Australians don't actually bury their dead. David showed us several places on sacred sites where the bones of relatives were laid to rest in rocky crevices above ground.

"Kangaroo meat is taboo to women of child bearing age," commented David while we were having lunch one day.

"Why is that?" asked Mary.

"Because the women get sick and the babies are born dead, blind or deformed," explained David.

"So women aren't allowed to have kangaroo meat from puberty to menopause," mused Mary.

"That's right; old women can eat kangaroo. Some research fellas found that if the meat isn't cooked right the parasites found in cysts in the meat hurt the developing babies. We figured that out a long time ago and made it taboo."

The next day we moved to the place of the Sweet Water Turtle. Each place we stayed at appeared more beautiful and majestic than the previous one. Below us was a large expanse of rock which created a small dam in the river with a waterfall spilling into a large pool of deep water. This was the place to catch turtles. David explained that to find the turtles, you look for bubbles rising in the water. I could feel the magic and peacefulness of this place transforming me in subtle ways.

*

Playful banter between the women led to several of us being given nicknames. Mary was dubbed Akela as she was the leader and we often behaved like unruly Girl Guides. I was called *Wide Mouth Frog* as everyone loved my version of the story. Sorry, I won't tell you the story here as it's the visuals that make it entertaining. Let's just say I have an ample mouth and ability to ham up a story graphically.

Diane always seemed to be on washing-up duty, her least favourite task at home, so her title was *She Who Washes Dishes*. When we taunted her, Diane would squat over the plastic tub, scrubbing the dishes violently as she leered at us, lifting her top lip to bare her teeth in a mock snarl. Being a larger-than-life personality, it was inevitable that Diane would score another nickname: *Sweet Water Turtle*. She had an uncanny ability to effortlessly manifest streams of bubbles in the water around her, just like her namesake.

40

One time we were still recovering from Diane's water turtle impersonations when Maggie let out a squawk. She had been standing shoulder deep in the water, nonchalantly flicking a leaf off her big toe into the muddy floor. As the tickling irritation continued she hauled herself onto the rocky edge for a closer look. There, firmly attached to her toe, was a slimy black leech as fat as my middle finger and ten inches long. The way Maggie reacted, you'd have sworn it was a vampire boa constrictor sucking the last drop of her life's blood! When we finally disengaged the beast, a glazed look of concern swept over Maggie.

"Oh my God! I'm naked! Are there any others on me?"

We all knew she was thinking, "Are there any others in me?" In a trice we were all out of the water, giving each other a leech search. Fortunately Maggie's innocence was intact.

With all the rock around it was easy to find a private place to lie down next to the water. I lay down in the afternoon sun and connected with the lizard energy and the earth, the baked rock warming me to my bones. My guides informed me that they would come to me that night and I needed to be ready. This request was not unusual, as I was often woken in the middle of the night and instructed to meditate.

*

We camped on the flat rocks high above the water. Jan as usual slept in the bush alone, and David was fifty meters away in the other direction. Mary, Diane, Maggie and I slept side by side like peas in a pod.

In the middle of the night, I guess around 3 am, I woke suddenly. My guides instructed me to get up. I presumed they wanted me to meditate quietly, so I stayed near the girls. I was instructed to stand up and hold a crystal in each hand.

"Now hold your arms out to the side and bring the energy down from the tenth level."

Raising my arms to shoulder height, I visualized a column of light coming down from the 10th chakra, 9th, 8th, 7th, as I had done so often before. WOW! This time something different, more physical, was happening! The energy coming down was so intense my knees started buckling with the pressure and I spontaneously started panting to cope with it.

"Keep your arms up and out to the side. Don't drop them!" I was ordered.

The energy felt like a lead weight on my head and arms. This was no meditation! The breathing through the chakras that I had practised was put to good use to bring the energy down. I panted noisily and heavily with the effort. It took every ounce of my strength and focus to bring the energy through my body and out my feet.

"Now place one crystal under each foot and hold your arms out to the side again."

I did as instructed. KERBOOM!! A surge of energy like a lightning bolt, ten times stronger than I had just experienced, rocketed down through me, activating the crystals and connecting them to the rocks beneath. My whole body felt as if it had exploded, like an orgasm that takes your head, fingers and toes off. The cells in my body pinged and crackled as the energy rippled through me.

I must have looked a sight to the three now wide-awake, dumbfounded women at my feet. I sweated, heaved and

42

panted above them like a grotesque vulture in the dark. I was oblivious to them. Still standing on the crystals with my arms outstretched, I was instructed to become the eagle and be as big as a mountain. On the inside way I flew over all the Kamali Council lands, spreading power and healing over the whole area. During this flight I transformed into the Dumby owl who is the messenger between the Wandjina and the Kimberley people. Once the energy had covered all the land area, I flew back.

My body and particularly my hands were radiating a powerhouse of energy of a magnitude I had not experienced before or since. I was instructed to go to David and give him the crystals as they belonged to his people now. One crystal was for the men's cave and one for the women's. Before I went to him, I placed my hands on Mary, Maggie and Diane in turn, giving them healing and dissipating the energy in my buzzing hands. Without speaking or explaining myself to my bewildered friends, I strode purposefully over to where David was sleeping. My experience was so real and physical, the instructions so clear, I had no doubts about the rightness of my actions.

I knelt beside David and gently woke him. As best I could, I explained what had happened and gave him the crystals. He looked up at the stars and asked where the Seven Sisters, the Pleiades were. I pointed them out to him. Fumbling for the right words to clarify the situation, I said "The same sky people, the Wandjina, who talk to you, also talk to me."

Somehow his Dreaming and mine were connected. I never in my wildest imagination would have guessed that this was what I had come to the Kimberleys for. I walked back over to my swag.

"What the hell do you think you are doing?" hissed Maggie in an incredulous whisper. "What's going on?"

I told the story again. We all chuckled profusely as Maggie demonstrated how ridiculous I looked and sounded as I channelled the energy down. Initially I had scared the hell out of them with my impersonation of an epileptic scarecrow. It was definitely not the best way to be woken up. Mary and Maggie were mortified that I had woken David, a respected Aboriginal elder.

Finally we settled down to sleep. I noticed that David had rekindled his campfire. He was sitting wrapped in a blanket and singing.

The next morning I felt nervous. The power and certainty of my nocturnal experience was giving way to self-consciousness and doubts. Who did I think I was? Fancy a brazen white woman waking up a law-keeper with wild stories of sky people and crystals!

David didn't say anything to me that morning. That was not his way – not respectful. Instead he spoke to Mary, the leader of our group. Mary told me later that David was a bit confused about what had happened in the night so he wanted to talk to me about it. My heart sank. Re-explaining to him in the cold light of day was going to be hard and scary. I felt that no matter how I told the story, it would sound trite, and its meaning and magic would be diminished. Would David understand? I silently asked myself. We got on with the day, knowing that when the time was right David and I would talk. In my heart I knew that what I had done was right and that what I experienced was extraordinary.

As we drove towards some new sacred sites, a frilled neck lizard stood sentinel, blocking the middle of the road and

44

compelling us to stop the car. Diane and I got out for a closer look. I had never seen one in the wild before. He stood rigidly to attention with his frill fully unfurled and mouth defiantly open. We eyed each other for a few minutes, then the lizard suddenly took off like a rocket.

David giggled like a little boy as he said, "You were lucky he didn't run straight up and over the top of you. They do that, you know." I think he was secretly disappointed that the lizard had deprived him of that entertainment.

Again there was the combination of water and large flat rocks at the next campsite, a women's water place. In contrast to the plentiful, alive, deep water of other places we had been, there were only shallow rock pools to swim in. No fresh water was flowing so the whole place felt less vibrant and slightly stagnant.

As the light was beginning to fade David showed us where the Wandjina Mejuk was incised into a large rock in the ground. He was an impressive 4.6 meters in length; the story is that Mejuk lay down in the earth so that the people could have life. Nearby was an enormous footprint forming a depression in the solid rock. I wondered how long ago it must have been that a human walked there creating the footprint when the ground was soft. David then taught us to sing to the setting sun.

In the middle of the night I woke up quickly, feeling alert and clear. This time I remained sitting as I brought the energy down through my chakras into the rocks beneath me. This experience was not overwhelming like the previous night. Just a light tingle rippled through. A bright light appeared in the sky, shining an intense beam from a single small cloud in an otherwise clear sky. I opened my eyes to look at it briefly then returned to my meditation. I saw a massive snake spirit, *Wungud*, move across the land like a river and the Wandjina man *Mejuk* rose up out of the ground and walked with it. I didn't know what to make of all this so I went back to sleep.

As we prepared breakfast everyone was commenting about the unusual bright light in the sky that had woken them during the night.

"The Wandjina man walked last night," David said. Everyone looked at him, hungry to hear more, but he didn't elaborate.

I stuck my neck out and told him, "I saw him and the snake."

"Yeah, the snake was there too," he concurred. I was overjoyed. It wasn't my imagination. He had experienced what I had.

After breakfast we walked to an initiation site. The whole area was flat and rocky with sparse vegetation. The stubble was blackened as if from a recent fire. At the site was a lone erect rock like a snake ready to strike. Nearby was a four-foot round, pregnant-looking rock with five small stones on it called the Wongai Creation Time women's rock. We noted the coincidence that there were five small rocks on it and we women were five in number.

David made a small fire next to the women's rock and got a branch from the same special tree used to smoke the caves two days before. He sang as he smoked each of us in turn, using the branch to waft the smoke around our bodies. He told the story of how Snake got jealous because the women had the Law, and sent a huge whirlwind to destroy them. The women put their heads down when the whirlwind came. The women kept their power but this place was bare because of the force of the whirlwind.

David's huge respect for women was evident in his treatment of us, and in his stories. "Women hold the power for the men," he said.

In another part of this bare area was a small pile of flat rocks. "This is where the boys get circumcised," explained David. "They dance and dance with their families until they are euphoric. Then they are circumcised and don't feel any pain."

We were led further on, to a lush waterhole with large, graceful trees and sandy banks. Now *this* was the women's waterhole and sacred place; I could feel it. I felt totally nurtured, refreshed and at peace there. David left us on our own for a few hours. What a celebration we had. We rolled over and over like logs, down the sandy bank into the water. I wiggled into the sand, enjoying its warmth. Mary gave me some Wasu, a Japanese water therapy where you are gently cradled and moved in the water like a baby. To surrender to such wonderful nurturing in a place so alive and feminine was blissful.

After our swim David took us through the bush to the other side of the waterhole. There, at the top of a rocky hill, was a small women's cave. He taught us how to clap as he sang and how to use our breath to send the power to Canberra to support his people's cause. At the time that we were in the Kimberley, an important battle was being waged in parliament for the land rights of David's mob. We unified our energies and thoughts. With much love and concentration we sent the message and the power.

We were quiet as we walked back, humbled by the honour of being invited to be a part of the ceremony. David took us back to the women's rock where he smoked our legs and sang again. After he had spoken out loud to his spirit ancestors, David translated for us.

"I was telling them that you are my sisters and aunties and that you sent the power and represented them because there was no one else able to do it for them."

(A state funeral for an important local Aboriginal man was held on that day, and most of the community was attending.) I was in tears at the thought that there were so few Aboriginal women left alive to do this ceremony. This was a very special day for me.

While the other women prepared a meal, David and I sat down to discuss the goings on of the other night. The power-sending ceremony made me realize that David knew that we respected and understood the essence of his Dreaming. I now felt he would be receptive to my story.

Taking a deep breath, I shared with him the key experiences which had led up to my coming to the Kimberley. He remained silent and attentive as I described what happened with the crystals, the energy surge and sending the power and healing over the land. I explained that one crystal was for the women's cave and one for the men's cave.

"I was only doing what I was instructed to do. I will understand if you and the elders don't want to place them there," I shrugged resignedly.

David spoke for the first time since we had sat down together. "This is big medicine; big magic."

He smiled as he looked down at the crystals in his hands.

*

The light and the colour of that country has to be seen to be believed. It is *Yorro Yorro*, everything standing up alive. I felt grounded, connected and timeless in this land. Each moment

48

and experience blended into one eternal now. David's stories wove into each other and the landscape, immersing me in the reality of the Dreamtime.

One day David sat in the shade with me and started talking. "You women are too noisy; too much hugging and touching each other. Our way is quieter."

I listened, enjoying the treat of David initiating a conversation with me. "See how we are sitting now?" David had sat at right angles to me so that if we both looked straight ahead we couldn't see each other's faces. "This is the respectful way to talk to your aunties and sisters. No eye contact."

Reluctantly we headed towards Derby, stopping once more at Manning Gorge. We were back with other campers again.

In the night Maggie shook me awake and whispered, "Is it time for the ceremony?"

I opened one eye, said sleepily, "What ceremony?" and closed it again.

Maggie nudged my dozing form and repeated the question.

I grinned and said, "This is my night off. If you need to do one it's your turn."

About fifteen minutes later Diane sat bolt upright in her sleeping bag and said, "When's the ceremony?"

Maggie and I chuckled. Diane and Maggie went off to the river to do women's business.

*

Arriving at Perth airport was a culture shock. We all felt like we were in a time warp. A sense of warmth, expansion and solidity buffered me and I silently sent David my thanks and deep appreciation for his wisdom. My thanks also went to Mary, for without her the trip would not have been possible.

I pondered on how synchronistic my life had become. It had not occurred to me that my body would be used as a veritable conduit for grounding the Light energy in the Earth and activating the programs in the crystals. The daily practice of bringing the energy down in a wide column and holding it for a period of time, the breathing meditation through the chakras, and the meditation of me becoming an eagle then becoming one with the land in a crystalline form, all made sense now. My trust in my guides had been validated with this profound experience in the Kimberleys.

I rang Wynelle in America and told her the story of the activation of the crystals and their new home in the Kimberley. Two weeks later, seven Galactic Wand shards arrived. Wynelle had dowsed that I should have them. I was amazed that I was now guardian of these beautiful crystals.

Soon after the crystal shards arrived, it occurred to me that others should have custodianship of some of them until the crystals' individual purposes became apparent. I was convinced that these crystals had a planetary purpose and were not for personal ownership. Kenneth, a Scottish friend with strong aboriginal connections, and Mary, Diane and Maggie were given one shard each. I gave one to Penny, but a few weeks later she gave it back, saying it didn't feel appropriate to have it. The remaining two crystals and the last third of the original Galactic Wand stayed with me.

Sai Baba Calls

Sathya Sai Baba came into my life through a book lent to me by my ex-mother-in-law's sister, whom I didn't have much contact with normally. One way or another, the universe will show you the next spiritual step if you stay open to it.

I found Samuel H. Sandweiss's book *Sai Baba, The Holy Man and the Psychiatrist*, fascinating. Soon after, another book about Sai Baba was lent to me. The more I read, the more I wanted to know about this man. What surprised me the most was my reaction; I was moved to tears several times reading both books, not so much from the content but from a soft energetic emanation gently urging my heart to open. Here was a small, afro-haired man in the south of India making a difference in the world and performing miracles of the calibre of Jesus!

The materializing of *vibhuti* (sacred ash) and jewellery was impressive, but to me the most awesome gift he had was his ability to inspire millions of people around the world to donate their skills and time in selfless service to others in need. I was amazed to learn that he had orchestrated the establishment of universities, schools, art and trade schools for both men and women, with free education. The construction of a hospital was under way, with free care made possible by local and international doctors and nurses donating their services for three months at a time. He was known to heal the sick and to have raised several people from the dead. There were many reports of his ability to materialize his physical form in several separate locations at the same time, to help and protect devotees in need.

All major religions have their main holy days celebrated at Sai Baba's ashram. Sai says, "There is only one God and man calls him by many names. Respect all religions – for none advocate breach of right conduct, values or morality."

Before long I discovered that there was a Sai Baba centre in Perth. I came home with several videos, which were avidly watched by Adam, Craig and me. I was seriously considering going to India to check him out. Not to do so seemed like being alive at the time of Jesus, hearing about the miracles, but not bothering to see for myself.

A surprise occurred when I discovered my friend Bev had gone the previous year to see Sai Baba with her neighbour Judy. Bev informed me that you don't decide to visit Sai Baba, you wait until you are called. Well he was certainly knocking on my door; but I couldn't say that I had a clear invitation yet.

When I returned the videos to the centre, I browsed through the various photographs of Baba and decided to buy one that I particularly liked. The volunteer behind the counter apologized, saying that it was the only one left and she couldn't sell it until more arrived. She suggested I buy one of the many other photos. I declined, saying that I would come back another day; for some reason I felt that this particular print was the one I should have.

At the back of the room four people were watching a video of Sai Baba. A man from this group had overheard our conversation, came over to me and quietly introduced himself. He had a copy of the same photograph that I wanted and offered me his. My first response was to refuse this stranger's generous offer. He pressed the photo insistently into my hands, saying that Sai Baba had signed it in his presence last time he was in India. I accepted his gift with gratitude. Sai's knocking was getting louder.

Not long after, I drove down south to Denmark, which is half an hour's drive from Torbay, to attend a group meditation. People from all over the world were meditating at the same time for world peace and planetary healing. I had participated in these world meditations ever since Jose Arguelles initiated the first Harmonic Convergence in August 1987. The gathering was on the granite rocks by the sea at William's Bay just outside Denmark.

As I drove under the canopy of majestic karri trees, I enjoyed the changing intensity of the dappled light. Bang! Out of the blue, Sai Baba's face materialized on the windscreen in front of me. I did a double take, shook my head and blinked, but the fuzzy-haired image was still there!

*

Sai Baba devotees kept popping up in the most unexpected places – his influence seemed everywhere. I travelled to Bridgetown to do a Brain Gym Balance for a little girl. During the session, which was in the family home, my attention was drawn to a photograph of Sai Baba pinned up on a bush pole in the room. Over a cup of tea we discussed the family's connection to Baba. The parents had taken their very ill daughter to India, to Baba, in the hope of a cure. Baba granted them a private interview, did some healing for the daughter and materialized some *amrita*, ambrosial nectar of the Gods.

I had never heard of *amrita*. The mother explained: "Years ago a murderous criminal fell at Baba's feet begging for forgiveness and Swami's grace. Sai Baba said that the only way he could redeem himself was to go to the town of Mysore and open an orphanage.

"The man protested that he had no money, no land; and who would entrust children to him anyway? Baba materialized a ring with a lid containing *amrita* and gave it to him. Like *vibhuti*, the *amrita* is said to have the power to heal with God's grace.

"Swami sent him away saying, 'Go to Mysore and trust.'

"This man followed his instructions. Everything miraculously fell into place, and to this day, the man still runs a large orphanage.

"The devotional room dedicated to Sai Baba has sacred ash, *vibhuti*, materializing all over pictures of Baba. *Vibhuti* and *amrita* are given to devotees who visit the orphanage. The story goes that no matter how much *amrita* is given away the container never runs out – in fact it refills while you watch!"

After sharing this story with me the mother left the room and came back with a tiny jar. "This is the *amrita* that Swami gave us. I would like you to have some."

"Thank you, but I can't accept it," I declined the gracious gift. "The little that you have left should be kept for those in need."

She insisted, saying, "It never seems to completely run out, and I know we wouldn't be having this conversation if you weren't meant to have some. It's for sharing, not hoarding."

I opened my hand and she poured a small pool of *amrita* into my palm. The nectar had a viscosity that was part-way between that of honey and maple syrup. The taste was subtle: not too sweet, and, when I rolled it around my mouth, something like roses.

A couple of months later Sai Baba appeared in my meditation, gave me a beautiful smile and handed me an envelope. The envelope contained money and written on the front of the envelope was one word – INDIA. Swami was finally calling me to come to him!

I drove to Bev's place in Nannup and asked her if she would go with me to India to see Baba. She agreed! Just as Baba had shown me, a lot of work came my way so I had ample money for the trip.

India

Although I was excited about visiting Sai Baba, I knew India would be challenging to me on every level, particularly in relation to the poverty, overcrowding and desperation of the people.

We travelled light, taking only what would fit into our backpacks. Our intention was to be away for six weeks, returning to Perth after celebrating Christmas at Sai Baba's ashram, Prasnanthi Nilayam, which means abode of eternal peace.

The first glitch occurred before we had even arrived in India. The flight from Perth to Singapore went smoothly. When we checked in to fly from Singapore to Madras we were told we weren't on the Air India flight as, according to them, we hadn't confirmed our flight! If we were unable to get on that flight we would be too late for our connecting flight to Bangalore.

I sent Reiki to the situation and Bev sent positive energy in her own way. Reiki is a form of healing where the practitioner becomes a channel through which the universal energy flows. This energy then flows from their hands to the client or the situation, healing them.

We rang Maggie asking her to send Reiki too. While I was Reiki-ing, Sai Baba appeared in my mind's eye, smiled and sprinkled *vibhuti* over the tickets. Again we went to the ticket counter and were turned away with a request for us to wait one hour.

An hour later we were asked to wait another five minutes. To say that we were getting edgy is an understatement. I did some more Reiki and Sai Baba appeared, shook his head at me and said, "Why are you bothering? It's all taken care of – TRUST!"

This time there were two tickets for us when we returned to the counter: not together, but on the same flight at least. Phew! Reiki of situations such as the flight to Bangalore and the arrangement of accommodation at the ashram quickly became the norm: our energetic insurance policy.

We rang Maggie with the good news, hastily thanked her for her help, then rushed to catch the plane. Mentally I thanked Baba and chuckled to myself with the realization that he was already testing me.

Our entry into India was deliberately gentle. We were met at the airport and driven to a clean hotel with lovely hot showers. The influence of the Raj was everywhere, from the chefs' outfits with large oversized white hats to the staff with bow ties and white gloves. The doormen were uniformed, with spectacular plumed headdresses. It was quite a contrast to the laid-back Aussie way of doing things.

We drove to Prasnanthi Nilayam at Puttaparthi in *God's Taxi*, as the Sai Baba devotee called his car. The way he drove, Bev and I were glad he had God on his side!

On the drive to Puttaparthi I meditated. In my meditation Sai Baba appeared in white robes and sat me on his swing. He affirmed that the main reason that I had come to India was to be in his presence and to learn three things:

- To learn humility and realize how far I had to go spiritually.

- To understand how far I have progressed.

- To reawaken faculties that I have had before in previous lives, but that had been shut down and the memory blocked in order for me to learn other lessons in subsequent lifetimes.

Swami told me that I was fortunate that I didn't need a private audience with him as I could connect with his energy at a distance and talk to him in my meditations.

At Prasnanthi Nilayam we secured floor space in shed number twenty three, sharing one long, open space with other female devotees. Apparently they have squeezed up to three hundred people in there when necessary! It cost fifty rupees for ten days' accommodation ($3.80 Aus. total).

Fortunately Bev knew the drill and whisked us off to buy mosquito nets and second-hand mattresses to insulate us from the concrete floor. To give us some privacy and delineate our boundaries, we strung up sarongs and scarves. It was like a colourful kid's cubby house.

At 4.30 am the next day we washed and went to Omkar Suprabhatan: the chanting of twenty one Oms. Bev and I ended up in the wrong queue. At 5 am we were sitting in the dirt in the queues for darshan which started at 6.45 am. Darshan means to see a great person and receive his blessing – literally, "To breathe the same air as". The group for the Oms and walking bajans, songs in praise of God, was further inside the mandir compound. The women were chanting Om with the men. Bev

58

and I joined in chanting with the others. A short while later the order came from Baba for all the women to shut up because we sounded like a pack of wolves!

The fact that we overheard the whispered message being relayed by servidals was not coincidental to us. Friends often affectionately referred to Bev, Maggie, Penny, Diane and me as the Wolf Pack. It seemed that it was Baba's way of letting us know that he knew we were here. It was my first go chanting at the ashram and already I was being told to shut up!

On our first day of darshan our line was placed sitting outside the main compound. To make it fairer, seating of the lines was decided like a raffle, with rows written on pieces of paper being selected one at a time from a bag. My first view of Sai Baba was fifty meters away from him. An aura of light around his head was visible to me even from that distance! At my second darshan I was stopped by security because I had a camera in my bag, and ordered to take it back to the shed. Fortunately my place was saved, but I lost Bev in the crowd of about ten thousand people. This time I was positioned in the eighth row, right near the gate through which Baba enters the compound, giving me a wonderful view of him.

My body felt quite rearranged, spacey and slightly fluey. My lower back ached for a couple of hours and then settled down. The men and women sat separately in darshan so that their attention could more easily focus on God and their spiritual development. This was also the reason that men and women slept separately at the ashram. My women's liberation attitudes were inflamed when I realized how much more time Baba was devoting to the men than to the women. I calmed down when someone told me that Sai believed that women were naturally more spiritual and devotional than men, so he spent more time helping the men.

I enjoyed the people around me each time I went to darshan. The Indian women were particularly tactile and would smile broadly at me as they stroked my hair and stared at my blue eyes. If someone left darshan early there would be a mad scramble to take that spot in order to get closer to Baba. We were squeezed in like sardines, with knees touching the people either side of us and our toes in the person in front's bottom, as we sat cross-legged for hours. Destitute lice-ridden beggars sat next to millionaires; everyone was equal here.

One time I was catapulted upwards like a cork out of a bottle by the force of the eager crowd. The servidals, whose role was to maintain order, commanded me to sit down.

"I'm trying!" I replied apologetically.

The women around me and I tried to muffle our laughter at the silliness of it all. I seriously wondered about the sanity of sitting cramped up in the dirt with thousands of others just waiting and hoping for a glimpse of Sai Baba.

Soon we settled into the ashram routine:

5.20 am	Omkar; Suprabhatan (chant Om 21 times)
5.35 am	Nagara Sankirtan (walking Bajans)
6.45 am	Darshan
Breakfast	20 minutes after Darshan.
9 am	Bhajans (Sacred songs in praise of God)
12-1 pm	Lunch
4 pm	Darshan
5.30 pm	Bhajans and meditation
6.45-7.45 pm	Dinner
9 pm	Lights out.

On 18th November I was elated by the presence of Sai Baba at darshan. The whole crowd had the most wonderful time with him that afternoon. We were all in his presence for about two hours continuously while he handed out thousands of saris to women. What a delight to watch!

He really played with the women. He threw saris to old women and gently scolded others too eager to get one. Baba gave one woman a sari, then gave her another and another and so on until she had twelve saris in her lap! The children loved this delicious joke. It was a truly festive atmosphere.

Being in Sai Baba's presence was all I needed. His love was all encompassing. I felt totally euphoric and peaceful. I then knew why I had come. Baba's energy field was so large that he was able to entrain and lift up the whole crowd's vibration just by his enlightened presence. There is an old saying, that a sage can alter the consciousness of a whole village simply by walking though it. On this day I was blessed with the opportunity to experience this first hand, with Sai Baba doing just that!

Our shed was full of interesting people from all walks of life and many different countries. We befriended an Argentinean woman called Marta who told us about an interview she had with Sai Baba. Two crippled Australians in wheelchairs were with her. Baba healed them in front of her and both walked from the interview fully recovered! We heard many first-hand accounts of miracles from devotees.

*

A few days later reality struck. I went to darshan feeling not so good. I couldn't face breakfast and all I wanted to do was lie down. Then the diarrhoea struck, and I began to throw up.

I nearly blacked out going to the toilet. Three Imodium tablets had no effect and I couldn't drink anything. Bev gave me some different tablets, which fortunately slowed everything down to a controllable state. It is amazing how quickly you become weak as a kitten with strange bugs racing around your intestines. During the few days when I was sick I had several intense dreams and meditations as I processed and integrated all that I was experiencing.

The toilet facilities for our shed of one hundred and fifty people consisted of four Asian squat toilets with a low tap in each – no toilet paper. At any given time at least one of the toilets wasn't working. It took me a few days to get acclimatized. The washrooms were four unpainted cement cubicles with a common open drain and a cold water tap in each, so a bucket was necessary to bathe yourself. There was nowhere to hang your clothes while you washed. The water went off at least twice a day at random. It was just too bad if it happened while you were in the middle of shampooing your hair or wanting to bucket-flush the toilet for the next person. The power went off about five times a day. Power blackouts were an everyday occurrence in India.

*

The size of the crowd swelled rapidly each day, as it drew close to Baba's birthday. During this time the Prime Minister of India and his political opponent were at Puttaparthi attending a three-day conference for National Unity. Sai Baba had both of them on a stage with him in a large hall at the ashram.

In Australia the term *"To give someone a serve"* means to tell them off or to speak up about something you don't like about that person or their actions. Well Sai Baba gave both political leaders a huge serve! This gave new meaning to Sai's saying,

"Love all, Serve all". He talked about the need for them both to proactively deal with corruption in India and work towards having fit water to drink for all Indians. At that time ninety percent of rural Indians did not have running water in their homes or clean water to drink.

Swami used the example of his hospital being free for poor people due to the donation of time and resources of the staff, to show them it was possible to change India. He then gave a long discourse on a range of subjects including the importance of not eating meat, smoking, or drinking alcohol.

On 23rd November, Sathya Sai Baba's birthday, Bev and I got up at 3 am and lined up for darshan, which was due to start at 8 am. That's right, five hours sitting in rows on the ground with several hundred thousand people from all over India and the world.

I passed the time praying my bladder and bowels would behave and practising to maintain my energy field and psychic space in the huge crowd. Apparently the following year, for Swami's seventieth birthday, there were two million people present.

Finally Baba arrived dressed in a white robe, escorted by a brass band and a procession of dancing children. Sai Gita, Baba's pet elephant, was by his side, decorated with flowers and beautifully embroidered covers. Sai Baba sat in his swing and everyone sang to him. Later he handed out balls of food, which to me tasted like sweet raw biscuit dough.

Mount Arunachala

With a couple of other Australian devotees, Robyn and Sunjay, we drove for eleven and a half hours to the Bhagavan Sri Ramana Maharshi ashram at Tiruvannamalai.

On the way we stopped at Bangalore and discovered that our Air India tickets to fly home from Madras had been cancelled, so we rebooked. After a wonderful meal at the Gateway Hotel, luxury after so much canteen food, we continued our journey.

Ramana ashram is at the base of Mount Arunachala, which is called the Pillar of Light by some people. Sri Maharshi spent many years at a time in silent retreat in a cave on Mt Arunachala. Apparently when he did speak, he was a master storyteller.

Ramana Maharshi's path to self-realization was to enquire, "Who Am I?"

> *Self-enquiry leads directly to self-realisation by removing the obstacles which makes you think that the self is not already realized.*
>
> *Sri Ramana Maharshi*

At the ashram meals were served on banana leaves on the cement floor and we ate with our right hands. Being left-handed, I would immobilize my left hand under my leg and eat with my right so that I didn't inadvertently offend anyone. The left hand is for ablutions and the right hand is for eating.

Sunjay, a bright teenager who lived semi-permanently with his grandmother at Sai Baba's ashram, had been blessed by eleven interviews with Sai Baba and had seen Baba manifest many presents for him over the years. With Sunjay as our youthful escort we scrub-bashed up the side of Mount Arunachala. There was no path and it was very rocky, but we had fun. Three quarters of the way up the mountain I saw a huge owl perched on a boulder in the full sun. When it spotted me it flew past my shoulder, reminding me of the Dumby owl and the Wandjina. My blue light guides chatted to me all the way up the mountain. I still had daily communication with them but they were taking a back seat, monitoring me while I immersed myself in India.

At the top a 360 degree view awaited us. Unfortunately, there was also a lot of smog partially obscuring the Hindu temple, one of the oldest temples in India, which lay at the foot of the mountain.

A ten-day Hindu Fire Festival was in progress on the top of Mt Arunachala, where a large metal vat 1.5 meters high filled with ghee burned twenty four hours a day. The rocks around the vat were covered in slimy black grease. The grease is sacred, and pilgrims to the top of the mountain have some grease placed on their third eye as a blessing by the men tending the fire. There were lots of wild monkeys all around. Judging by the smell of the grease I am sure it had its fair share of monkey poo in it. However, not daunted, we did as the locals did and allowed ourselves to be anointed. Sunjay, Bev and I then sang the Gayatri Mantra, a universal prayer, three times:

Om bhur bhuva sva;
Tat savitur varenyam
Bhargo devasya deemahi;
Dheeyoyona prachodayat
Om shanti; shanti; shanti.

A steady stream of Hindus came up a well-beaten path which started near the ancient temple. Although Bev and I were glad we had found our own way up the other, more pristine side of Mt Arunachala, we were grateful to take the easier well-trodden route back down.

After four fascinating days in Tiruvannamalai, Robyn, Sunjay, Bev and I headed back to Puttaparthi.

Karmic Burn-off

Bev and I bought Indian Airline tickets which allowed us to travel all over India for three weeks. The night before we flew the first leg to Bombay things came to a head for us. We were both feeling out of sorts and miraculously were able to telephone Maggie and get through.

Maggie said she would send Bev some Reiki so Bev lay down to receive some distance healing. At this time Bev was new to "all this Reiki stuff" and was amazed at the intensity of the energy coursing through her body a few minutes later. She felt hot and electric, so I held her feet to help anchor the energy. The distance Reiki was so impressive that Bev vowed to herself that she would learn Reiki when she went home. She is now a Reiki Master.

People talk about Puttaparthi and Sai Baba causing you to put apart your "I" or ego (Putt – aparth – I). Well, that process began in earnest that night, and continued for the whole of the rest of my stay in India. In fact it took me months to put the bits back together. It was like an intense psychic death.

The humility lessons Baba had promised me came thick and fast. Bev was my Humility Fairy, letting me know when I was being arrogant, condescending or controlling. I felt as if I had been run over by a Mac truck – not by Bev, but by the force of Sai Baba behind the experiences. I was shown all the little ways I stole other people's thunder and didn't allow them to have their day. For example, when we were at Baba's ashram there was a lovely human angel who cleaned our toilet block. She was very friendly, always smiling and gracious. She was inspirational to Bev and me. Bev wrote lovely sentiments to this woman on a thank you card and intended to give it to her with a pen. I said I would like to add some money to the present. As I was last to write on the card, I handed it to the woman and we both thanked her.

I thought nothing more of this until Bev brought the subject up as an example of my behaviour a week later. I had taken control, stolen her idea, her gift and power by giving the card to the lady as if Bev was just tagging along. I was mortified! She was right. The most distressing thing was that I had been oblivious to the effect my actions had on Bev.

On 30th November we flew to Bombay. The polluted air was thick, smelly and stinging to our eyes. The desperation of the people was much worse, or at least was more obvious, than in the country. Trucks came by to collect food for the needy from the garbage bins of a restaurant across the road from where we were staying. A young woman with a couple of toddlers and a baby at her breast rummaged through rubbish in the hope of finding scraps for her children. The children's clothes were in tatters.

One morning I saw a man emerge from his home which was a few pieces of corrugated iron leaning precariously against each other, like a humpy on the side of the road. His hair was shining and neatly combed, his white shirt and grey trousers were beautifully pressed, and his shoes were polished. He looked like a well-to-do businessman with his attire and briefcase. If I hadn't seen it with my own eyes, I would never have believed that this man lived in a lean-to. He didn't have much, but he carried himself with dignity.

My sense of powerlessness and frustration in the face of so much destitution caused my behaviour to seesaw wildly. One moment I was consciously paying too much for things in an attempt to help the person, the next I was holding on fearfully to every cent and perceiving everyone as corrupt. One beggar angrily pushed me when I followed Swami's suggestion to offer to buy food for the woman and her baby, rather than give her money.

I adored the magnificent colours of the women's saris. My eyes drank them in like a parched man at an oasis. The colours of their clothes were vibrant, varied and utterly refreshing. As I love wearing bright colours I would have bought some saris, but visions of me treading on the hem and having the yards of material unravelling out of control and falling around my ankles, prevented me from doing so.

Bev and I decided to change our flight to Udaipur to a day earlier so that I could celebrate my birthday somewhere more restful than Bombay. We phoned Indian Airlines at 10 am to reschedule our flight to that day, 1 December. They waitlisted us and we were instructed to go to the airport in the hope that two seats would become available. On the way to the airport I sent Reiki to the situation then asked Sai Baba to arrange tickets for us. I handed it all over to him, trusting that whatever was right for us would happen. At 11.40 am we arrived at the airport.

Waiting interminably in queues is a part of life in India. I queued in one line to get our airline tickets and Bev was in another. Eventually it was our turn and we were told that both of us were in the wrong queues and we had to go to checkout number ten.

As we waited in line at checkout ten Bev told me that bribes were the way to get business done in India. I didn't feel right about it and asked her to get the tickets by normal means. I tuned into Sai Baba and saw him standing with two tickets in one hand, and tapping them on his other hand. I figured the tickets were available but Sai was holding out for some reason.

Bev handed over our tickets. The attendant asked us to wait five minutes and left us at the counter. While he was away Bev whispered that she had put a bribe of fifty rupees in with the tickets.

"If you truly trust that everything is in divine right order and you hand it over to God, you don't need to bribe people," I said in frustration.

Bev replied, "In India you have to play the game, and bribes have worked for me here before."

I countered this with, "If we want to move to the next level spiritually we must be in integrity. What was okay before is not okay as you become more conscious and responsible. When you start to wake up spiritually, you can't go back to sleep. It gets too uncomfortable."

The ticket officer returned, opened our tickets and noticed the money. "What's this?" he said laughing, "You have learned a lot about India!" He called over four other airport officers and they all laughed at Bev and me. Bev was as embarrassed as hell. The man handed back the money and asked us to go to another line that was finally the correct one for waitlisted people.

While we waited yet again I checked in with Baba on the inside way. He kissed my ticket and handed it to me, then kissed Bev's ticket twice and handed it over. I knew then that we would get on the flight even though it was already midday; there were seven people on the list before us and the plane was due to fly out at 12.30. When we arrived at our lovely little hotel in Udaipur the manager told us that our flight had been delayed. It usually left at 11am. If it hadn't been delayed I would have been stuck in Bombay for my birthday. Thank you, Sai, once again!

From then on Bev called me her Integrity Fairy, and she continued to be my Humility Fairy.

Due to the intensity of the lessons I was learning I became ill as I attempted to keep pace with all the processing that was happening on inner levels. My nose ran like a tap. My brains felt as if someone was smashing them against rocks like the washing down by the river. During this time I received an image of Sai Baba showing me reams of paper like a long scroll, which was a metaphor for the long list of things that I needed to learn or clear. The lined paper went blank as I watched, and Sai informed me that all would be resolved by the end of my birthday.

The 2nd December was my birthday and I felt terrible! I had hardly slept at all due to a very high fever causing my brain to feel cooked. I wore thick socks, thermal underwear and a jumper to bed. The two blankets I put over my sleeping bag were not enough to keep me warm even though the weather was hot and humid. All my bones and joints ached, but particularly my feet. Several past life memories came up vividly during this time. It truly was a karmic burn-off.

My friend Susie had given me an envelope when I left for India, with the instruction to open it on my birthday. It contained a lovely card and an eagle feather. It was so thoughtful of her and I was feeling so poorly, it made me cry. Bev gave me a framed picture of Mt Arunachala and a hollow rock with a tiny cave of crystals inside it. It was definitely a boy rock and had a face in it like Casper the friendly ghost. As it had so much personality we named the rock Bombay.

We postponed my birthday celebrations until I was feeling better. Miraculously the karmic burn-off was complete by the next day. My health was reviving and I felt like I might live after all.

That evening we went to the Lake Palace Restaurant, which was on a tiny island in the lake. It was opulent and beautiful, with walls of marble inlaid with lapis lazuli and other precious stones. After a sumptuous buffet dinner we watched a puppet show and traditional dancing with live music. At the end of the show the dancers invited me up to the stage to dance with them. I had a ball, twirling and dancing with them, with a huge grin on my face.

A few days later Bev and I flew on to Jodhpur, then caught the overnight train to Jaisalmer. As both of us were feeling fragile, intestinally speaking, we decided to buy first-class tickets so we could collapse and sleep safely ensconced in our own private quarters. When we got on the train there was a young European couple in our two-berth room. They insisted it was their room. Bev and I looked at each other wanly. We barely had the strength to stand up and needed an argument like we needed a hole in our heads.

Bev and I dragged ourselves along to the next compartment,

where ten people were crammed into a four-berth cubicle. Without saying a word to each other we returned with renewed determination to confront our invaders. The couple was as resolute as we were, self-righteously standing their ground. Finally as the train was taking off, a ticket collector came to our rescue, determined that it was indeed our berth and asked the couple to move on.

The train was a relic from the 1940s with enormous light switches, an old-fashioned clattering fan and a heavy metal sliding door for security and privacy. As I slid the door closed the whole monstrous thing fell off its rollers into my hands. Bev and I looked at each other incredulously then collapsed in a heap laughing, with the door on top of us. We lifted the door back on its track and went inside – so much for security! Exhausted, we had a fitful night's sleep. At each stop the familiar call for hot chai, sweet spiced tea, echoed through the night.

Jaisalmer is near the border with Pakistan. We had great fun on a camel and jeep safari into the desert. Riding in the back of an open jeep, we rapidly became unrecognisable under a thick coating of yellow dust. Profuse sweating encrusted the dust on our bodies and even our teeth. We looked like bedraggled extras for *Lawrence of Arabia*.

The first stop was a village of untouchables. This is a derogatory term for people of the lowest caste in India. Mahatma Gandhi was the first person to effect changes to the rigid caste system by demanding the eradication of "untouchability". His efforts led to the "people of God", as he preferred to call them, being given permission to attend Hindu temples.

In the middle of nowhere the government had built houses and a school for the village. There was barely a tree or bush in sight, only dust, sand and rocks. A twelve-year-old boy helped me onto my camel then climbed up and sat behind me. I asked my driver if he went to school. He proudly told me, "No. I am a working man now."

I felt at home on the camel, enjoying its rolling gait. The ride lasted an hour, finishing with a magnificent sunset over the sand dunes while musicians played and sang. I was glad that our tourist trip was providing some income for these ostracized people. We certainly had a colourful time and returned to our hotel tired, filthy and happy.

At another desert village where the temperature is often fifty degrees centigrade, weaving was demonstrated. Curiously it was Australian merino wool that was mixed with Indian wool and woven into shawls with local designs. The quality of the weaving was excellent, and it distressed me that these people were paid so poorly and lived in such inhospitable surroundings.

The next day we visited some beautifully preserved Jain temples with intricate sandstone carvings. In the hills above Jaisalmer are cenotaphs, the tombs of rulers and maharajas. Our tour guide told us that when a maharaja died his four to six wives were thrown onto the funeral pyre with him to keep him company in the afterlife. It was a case of jump into the flames or be thrown in.

I indignantly asked him, "If the first wife died before the maharaja, did he jump onto her funeral pyre?"

He looked at me as if I was totally insane and replied, "Of course not!"

Jaisalmer is a maze of narrow streets constantly flowing with processions of people celebrating festivals and weddings, creating an air of exotic mystery. Many of the houses are decorated with intricate wooden carvings around the windows and on the doors. One of my favourite memories of this city is hooning through the rabbit warren of narrow lanes at night on the back of a tiny scooter. The owner of a carpet shop offered to give us a ride back to our hotel, as he was concerned for our safety at night. I don't know how the three of us managed to squeeze onto the seat and stay on as we ducked and weaved through animals and people in the dark.

"Don't you dare let go of him!" Bev cried as she clung tightly to my waist. There was more of Bev hanging off the end of the scooter than on it.

In tag–team style, Bev took her turn to come down with vomiting and "the runs" on the trip back to Jodhpur. By now our early morning conversations were reduced to discussing the state of our stomachs and bowels. Playing tourist in Rajasthan gave our bodies time to catch up with the massive changes and clearing that we were experiencing on every level.

From Jaisalmer we flew to Delhi and on to Agra to see the Taj Mahal and other tourist spots. By now Bev was a picture of misery, as she had broken out in cold sores which completely covered both lips and encrusted both nostrils. According to Louise Hay, cold sores are associated with "festering words and fear of expressing them". Bev and I discussed this idea, as the outbreak of cold sores was so extensive and severe.

I had never experienced Bev being as angry towards me as she had been the morning we set off for Bombay. We both felt that this incident may have been the trigger for Bev's cold sores. I sensed that her outburst had frightened Bev and ever since she had held back her words for fear of another explosion.

*

In Varanasi, with the opportunity to sleep more, Bev began to recover. At 4.45 am, a few days after we arrived, we took a rickshaw ride to the ghats on the shores of the Ganges River. We wore scarves and blankets to ward off the early morning cold.

It was totally foggy so at 6.45 we returned to our hotel, passing a long line of women walking to the ghats with sacks containing provisions on their heads. This was the time of year to take a pilgrimage to all the major temples, ending at the sacred Ganges River. This walk for the women was the end of a seven-day journey. Soon after, we passed five men literally walking backwards all the way to the last stop in their pilgrimage.

The next day at 6.30 am we returned to the ghats. This time there was a light mist. The full moon was still visible and glowing brightly. A fourteen-year-old boy rowed us up and down the river as we took in the amazing spectacle before us. It was a fantastic synthesis of everything that India is.

I saw a man dressed in saffron robes, an enormous japamala (string of prayer beads) with beads as large as ping pong balls around his neck and a tiger skin draped across him. His black hair was thickly matted in dreadlocks and was long enough to sit on.

Sewerage pipes emptied straight into the river right next to people doing laundry on stone slabs. They slapped the clothing down, then kneaded it like bread. The washing was spread out on the rocks to dry, creating a huge colourful mosaic.

Hundreds of men and women were bathing, performing puja, meditating and praying or doing yoga at the water's edge. Marriages and cremations happened side by side here. There is an electric crematorium but many opt for the open-air, wood-fuelled pyres. The relatives come to the Ganges to pray and bathe for ten days after the ashes of the deceased are offered to the river. Only men attend the funerals. If there are no male relatives the women are permitted to come.

The bodies of those who are considered to be "of God" are not cremated but are offered as they are to the river. These are sadhus, babies, pregnant women, people bitten by cobras (Shiva) and people with leprosy. A sadhu is a holy person who is striving for enlightenment, and is usually addressed as Swamiji or Babaji. The corpse of a tiny baby wrapped in cotton and tied to a slab of wood floated past our boat.

The sun rose orange-pink, reflecting on the glassy flat river. A peace descended on me with a sense that what I was observing was perfect: the fecundity, the frenzy, the death and the religious rituals. In this moment I stopped wrestling with India.

Bev bathed an initiation rock belonging to Maggie in the river. She had lovingly taken this egg to every sacred site on our journey. We collected some bottles of Ganges water to take back to Sunjay and Robin, then we sang the *Gayatri* and *Loka Samasta*:

> *May the denizens of the Earth*
> *Find peace and happiness*
> *Om Peace Peace Peace*

> *Loka Samasta*
> *Sukino Bavantu*
> *Om Shanti Shanti Shanti*

*

The whole trip had been miraculous and transformational, but the process was harrowing, so we decided to come home early. Before we flew home Bev and I wanted to have one more day at Prasnanthi Nilayam. From Bangalore we drove in *God's Taxi* to Put-aparth-I. As we drove through the gates of the ashram a huge owl flew past my window.

On this last day I prayed for four things:

- For Sai Baba to look into my eyes and be close enough that I could feel his energy strongly.

- To see him materialize something at close range (it didn't have to be for me).

- To feel his presence in my heart and to be more loving as a result.

- And, of course, to have an interview.

We arrived just in time for Omkar. The men sounded so reverent and peaceful chanting the 21 oms. The women followed the men as they walked around the ashram singing bhajans (Nagara Sankirtan).

At darshan we were about the sixth row to file in so we were placed next to the old women, centre front of the mandir and eight rows back. Oh joy! This was the most plum position for a woman in the whole area, giving me a perfect view of the whole proceedings. Some people left to prepare for a wedding inside the mandir so I was able to move forward to the third row.

Baba walked by and manifested *vibhuti* right in front of me. I had a clear view of the whole process. He placed his hand palm downwards and circled it in the air. I could see his palm was empty as we were sitting on the ground below him. Sai closed his hand and sprinkled *vibhuti* into the open hands of three women in the front row directly in front of me.

Sai Baba then went inside the mandir to conduct the wedding. Everyone waited patiently for one and a half hours. When he reappeared Baba threw sweets to the children and blessed them.

Just before bhajans the woman in front of me whispered a warning to me that she was going to join the choir, so that I could quickly take her place in the second row. A little while later the woman in front of me also left, and I found myself in the front row, centre stage!

The last song sung at bhajans was my favourite, Loka Samasta, which I had sung every day while in India. My heart filled with joy. After bhajans, Sai walked slowly past the children, gently touching them on the head and allowing them to briefly touch his hands. He looked in my direction and momentarily our eyes connected. His eyes were soft and unconditionally loving. As he left the compound Sai passed me, so close I could have touched him. As he did so, he looked directly at me again.

For lunch at Sai Towers I had a baked jacket potato with real butter! I had just the day before said to Bev that a baked potato was the food I was most hanging out for when I got home. After writing Christmas cards for the many friends we had made at the ashram we set off to find Robyn.

We found her with a choir of men and women singing Christmas carols in one of the sheds. It made my heart full and I was all teary singing *Noël*. I was going to miss celebrating Christmas with thousands of devotees from all around the world.

Robyn magnanimously gave Bev and me *vibhuti* that Baba had given to her in an interview. So indirectly I even got my interview. We gave Sunjay and Robyn the water from the Ganges and said our goodbyes, grateful for these wonderful people who had touched our lives. It was a perfect day, and I had received everything that I had asked for. True to his word, Sai Baba had delivered on all three things he said I had come to India to experience. I had certainly learnt about my many shortcomings.

The challenges presented to me in India, had forced me to use my intuition and spiritual guidance continuously. The messages I was receiving proved to be accurate and I had learned to trust them.

The lifetime that Baba alluded to that I was ready to remember, was a lifetime in 1370 AD in Northern India. I was an ascetic who lived in a cave fashioned into a single room with a dirt floor, and no window or door. I slept on a low, wooden-framed bed with a woven cloth lattice as the base (charpoy). It had no mattress, pillow or blankets. I wore a loincloth (dhoti) and a turban. In winter I had a woollen shawl. As I ate only one meagre meal a day, I was very skinny. Spending thirteen to fourteen years alone, my spiritual practices were disciplined and my life austere. I experienced deep inner peace and had many visions of the future.

Unfortunately the rigid adherence to my spiritual practices and my separation from the rest of humanity became a blockage to my next level of evolvement: bliss and joy. I had missed the point – I needed to embrace and celebrate life, not deny it. Peace and contentment were there, but no joy or unconditional love in sharing with others and acknowledging god within all people. I think it is easy to be spiritual, isolated in a cave, although it has its challenges. The acid test is to *be* what you have learnt in the bustle of everyday life.

> *There is only one religion* ... *the religion of love*
> *There is only one caste* ... *the caste of humanity*
> *There is only one language* ... *the language of love*
> *There is only one God* ... *and He is omnipresent*
>
> *Sai Baba.*

Dolphin Healing

I was depressed at the thought of going home on Christmas Eve to an empty house and no food in the fridge; family is what Christmas is all about. As I had intended to be away, my sons were in Adelaide celebrating Christmas with their father, and my niece Katie had gone to Nepal with Paul.

I gave myself Reiki healing and called in Sai Baba. To my surprise Sharky came in instead! Sharky is a wonderful wild dolphin I had connected with in Bunbury, a city south of Perth. I could feel and see Sharky's presence, his warmth and joy, soothing and nurturing me. I had never had a live dolphin psychically visit me before! Sharky stayed with me until the depression dispersed. I went to sleep with a smile on my face, feeling loved and happy. We flew home the next day.

Always the magnanimous and thoughtful one, Maggie invited me to have Christmas with her family. I had a delightful day and everyone made me feel at home.

Three weeks after returning to Perth, I decided to visit the Bunbury dolphins. I had waded with them a couple of times previously at the Dolphin Centre. The contact with Sharky in India had such an impact on me that I want to physically reconnect with him. Someone had told me I could swim freely with the dolphins at the two groins where the river meets the sea. I resolved to find the place.

I arrived at the river mouth at 7.30 am. I walked to the end of the groin, donned my wet suit and snorkelling gear and sat down. Using Reiki I tuned into the dolphins.

"Phew! Phew!" A dolphin surfaced and breathed just below me. Several other dolphins surfaced, then swam to the other side of the rivermouth to surf the waves breaking on the sandbar there.

With gusto I jumped into the water and swam over to them. The current was sucking water into the river so I had to swim strongly and consistently to get across. The water on the other side of the far groin was still and clear. The buoyancy of my wetsuit, without a weight belt, allowed me to half sit and lounge on my back like an otter. From this vantage point I could leisurely look for dolphin fins, hoping that they would swim over to me.

Yahoo! Here they came! I floated on my tummy in snorkelling position with anticipation. I was not prepared for what happened next. Six large dolphins slowly approached and surrounded me. I lay on the surface of the water, looking down and around at them, feeling perfectly safe. Two lay side by side to the right of me. Two dolphins lay mirror fashion to my left. One lay belly-up on its back directly beneath me. The sixth dolphin floated on its tummy ahead of me so that its face was only fifteen to thirty centimetres away from my face.

I was astounded! *I had wall-to-wall dolphins encasing me, so close I could touch them!*

The visibility was excellent, and we were in about three meters of calm water. When I took a breath and went below the surface they held formation, cocooning me as I swam. I floated motionless, dying to touch one of them but not willing to risk shattering the special moment. Occasionally one would swim off momentarily for air then resume its position.

Still in the same positions, the dolphins gave me a sonar bath, making my forehead tingle and buzz with its intensity. They were healing me! My health was still shattered after India and I had learnt some big lessons which I was still integrating. The dolphins must have read my energy field and decided to help me.

I have never known dolphins to lie hovering like that, completely enveloping a person. This healing embrace lasted uninterrupted for fifteen minutes, although it felt like half an hour. I was laughing and crying at the same time. There was so much love and joy being radiated to me as they clicked and whirred. All six dolphins were within arm's reach the whole time.

When they could hear me laughing into my snorkel, they stopped and zoomed over to the sand bar to surf the waves. They were as ecstatic as I was and put on a show just for me, as I clapped and cheered. One dolphin did a full circle in the air before splash-landing. Another surfed on a wave, using the momentum to shoot high in the air, flying three and a half meters before diving in. Others did spiralling twirly-whirlies and back flips. I was euphoric!

The dolphins interacted with me more "normally" from then on. I duck-dived and swam along with one, who slowed his speed to keep pace with me. A mother brought her baby for me to admire. These brief interactions and swims past me were more what I was used to.

For two hours I swam and played alone with these dolphins. Finally, tired and cold, I left the water as the pod swam off to feed. I am deeply grateful for the healing activation they blessed me with.

Something fundamental changed for me with this interaction. The communication with Sharky in India, and the sonar bath which the six Bunbury dolphins had honoured me with, firmly established a telepathic link between us.

Reiki Magic

A Vedic astrologer told me that, in mid-1995, I would meet the "man of my life".

"He will be someone who will open my heart," I shared with Diane. We discussed the idea of a new partner for me while we had a late afternoon stroll in the forest. The full force of the summer day's heat was waning and the crickets were making a racket. "I hope the astrologer is right. I feel ready for a new relationship."

As I finished speaking, a cloud of approximately forty monarch butterflies lifted out of the grass at my feet and swarmed around me. Diane looked at me in amazement. A spiralling mass of vibrant orange and black butterflies fluttered over my body. In that magical moment I knew without a doubt that within the next two months I would meet my next partner.

From that moment on, monarch butterflies have symbolized that my love is thinking of me.

*

Sheahara, the Canadian "Love Bunny" as I affectionately call her, came into my life via Maggie. Both women are excellent

Reiki masters who trained with Phyllis Furamuto in the United States. Sheahara has a unique way of using Reiki, which has profound results. Reiki haircuts are her specialty. You focus on what you want to release or draw into your life as she does Reiki on your head and shoulders. Then she cuts and trims off the resistance and limitations preventing you from having what you want. Boy, do these haircuts work!

It was January 1995, and I told Sheahara that I didn't want to wait five or six months for this man the astrologer had told me about. "I want to meet him this week," I said emphatically. I focused on the type and quality of relationship I wanted as Sheahara channelled the Reiki energy. It was the best haircut I had had in a long time. That was Monday.

Mid-week, Sheahara and I went down to Bunbury to visit the dolphins. We slept on the beach in front of the Dolphin Centre. That night I had a dream about a middle-aged Greek man rescuing me from a hospital and opening my heart. This dream told me that someone very healing for me was coming into my life. I could feel him getting closer.

After waiting in vain for two hours at the Dolphin Centre, we drove to the groins to look for the dolphins. They were there! As I entered the water two dolphins came close to me but didn't stay long.

Sheahara was not a strong or confident swimmer. Gingerly she entered the water, but the dolphins swam further out. She returned to the rocks and sat on the water's edge. A small dolphin surfaced next to the rocks where she was sitting. Sheahara squealed and clapped with girlish delight at the sight of her first wild dolphin.

The following Sunday I was invited by a friend, Raylene, to watch a video of a workshop by Alton, a channel and meditation teacher. When I arrived on Sunday morning I found Diane propped against the kitchen sink, chatting to a striking lanky man. He had the most beautiful, open aura about him. I was introduced to Tony and without hesitation I asked him if I could give him a hug. I knew this man. I knew his energy although it was the first time we had been introduced.

I asked, "Where have you been all my life?" (Now where on Earth did that corny line come from? It was out of my mouth before I could think!)

Without hesitation he looked at me and said, "Waiting for you."

Tony sat between Diane and me on the sofa to watch the video. When we did a guided meditation with Alton, the three of us held hands. This video and meditation was a turning point in all three of our lives. Diane, Tony and I continued on the same spiritual path, remaining steadfast friends from this point on.

With the video was a colour chart of the twelve chakras. The **tenth** chakra was a **pale ice-blue** and was labelled the **intergalactic gateway**! This was the first time that I had confirmation outside myself of the validity of the blue light and the tenth level, which I had used in my meditations for the past two years.

The following week Sheahara, Diane and I were invited to a party at Raylene's house. Tony was there, and it was apparently quite comical watching the two of us trying to pretend there was no chemistry between us. We sat next to each other after the meal. Diane, who was sitting opposite, teased us about the sparks flying and energy mixing in our auras above our heads. Ten days after our first meeting, we went on our first date, talking incessantly until 3 am.

Within two months we were living together. This was the first time in my life that I had a partner with the same spiritual and philosophical interests as myself.

*

A few months before he met me, Tony had suddenly developed an interest for all things native American. He painted a cowhide with sacred Indian symbols, completing it just before we met. This subsequently became our meditation mat – our spaceship, as he called it.

We discovered that one of the most positive lifetimes we had had together so far was a life as Indians in the British Columbian area of Canada in 1200 BC. He had been my father and teacher. Unconsciously he had painted the hide as a way of reconnecting with that time.

I have been doing past life regressions since 1978. Over time this has led to my combining Kinesiology and regression techniques into a powerful healing tool. Since 1993 I have been teaching these skills in my Cellular Memory Integration workshops. It was therefore natural that many past life memories began to surface for Tony and me.

The last lifetime that Tony and I shared was during World War Two, when we were married to each other and had three children. As a consequence, we felt we were still married to each other in this life, so saw no point in officially marrying again. It was curious that we felt like a solid couple from the first moment we moved in together. It was very easy and natural, with none of the usual teething trouble. We brought magic, love and gratitude into each other's lives.

Before Tony and I moved in together, several big black crows would daily wake up Tony by cawing loudly at the bedroom window. One morning, they became so persistent it annoyed him. I suggested that they might have a message for him. Tony initially thought I was teasing him. I encouraged him to close his eyes and see if he could get a message. To his surprise Tony received immediately, "Look for my brothers and look for the fallen eagle." It made no sense to him or me, but I asked him to write it down. It would be many months before this message would have any meaning for us. From that moment, ravens and crows became Tony's animal guides.

*

Diane, Tony and I attended one of Alton's meditation workshops. We were fascinated that we could actually see light beings around Alton and sometimes we saw these beings physically enter or overlay themselves on him. At this workshop we learned about Drunvalo Melchizedek's work with sacred geometry, his Flower of Life meditation and their connection to an ancient Egyptian mystery school.

Tony and I sponsored Patricia Athena and Lloyd Taylor to teach The Flower of Life meditation techniques in Perth. They had both trained with Drunvalo and qualified as teachers. This was the most powerful and catalytic workshop I had attended for many years. The friendship between Tony, Diane and me seemed to ignite and accelerate our individual personal and spiritual growth. It was at this time that I gave Tony the Galactic Wand shard that Penny had returned to me.

*

One afternoon, while Sheahara was staying with me, my sister Barbara dropped in for a chat. Over a cup of tea at the

89

kitchen table Barbara, my son Adam and Sheahara chatted about what Reiki was. By the time Barbara left to go home both she and Adam had booked in to do a Reiki One class with Sheahara. That night I rang my other son, Craig, who was living in Adelaide. When he found out his brother and auntie were doing Reiki he sighed and said he wished he could go, too. I gave him my frequent flier points so that he could fly home for the weekend to attend the Reiki workshop. Although my boys had attended meditation and personal development courses as teenagers, this was the first time they had expressed interest in learning any healing.

The Reiki class of fifteen students was held in my friend Terrie's beauty therapy clinic. Sheahara and another Reiki master, Joel, had a natural flow to their co-teaching. The class was relaxed, enjoyable and informative. I had already learnt Reiki Two at the time, so I went along to support. Adam had had a fall and broken his arm the night before the class, but even with a cast on his right forearm he was still keen to attend. We paired up, linking arms around each other's waists, so that Adam could use his one good arm while I provided the other hand.

After this combined effort Terrie, who was receiving, said, "Patti, you've got good energy in your hands, but Adam's is ten times stronger than yours." Adam was very pleased with this comment. When my mother later received Reiki from Adam and Craig she also commented about how much stronger and warmer the energy from both their hands was compared to mine.

Monkey Mia

On 21 March 1995 Katie and Sheahara received a message from their guides that my third piece of crystal had to go to Monkey Mia near Shark Bay, and Sheahara had to go with me to connect with the dolphins there.

I sat down and meditated to see if this was appropriate for me. The following is a transcript of the information my guides gave me:

> There are grids of energy in the Earth's crust and in the seabed all over the world which are being activated and realigned with the electromagnetic grid set up around the Earth in space.
>
> The magnetic shifts that people have been talking about and experiencing are part of this. This realignment will not be too devastating because so many people are waking up now and healing their patterns.
>
> The grid-work energies under the sea are being activated by extraterrestrials. Many humans are helping to align the land ones. Patti, you are to help with the ocean ones. The crystals are part of the Earth's alignment and healing.
>
> The third crystal piece needs to go to Monkey Mia.

Monkey Mia is eleven hours' non-stop driving, north of Perth, on the coast in the middle of nowhere. In spite of this, thousands of people from all over the world go there to commune with the wild dolphins who practically beach themselves in order to interact with humans. It is really special to see long lines of people of all ages and nationalities being enlivened and opened up by this contact.

The previous year I had stayed at Monkey Mia for a week with my friend Susie. We had hired a large army tent with its own toilet and shower attached at one end, a two-burner gas cooker and a little fridge. Catching the bus up enabled us to bring up boxes of food. Susie and I walked for hours each day, played with the dolphins and relaxed in the hot thermal spring tub in the evenings. There is nothing to do there except relax and rest.

One day Susie got it into her head that her pet amethyst crystal needed to go for a walk. This was not a stone that fitted neatly in one hand. Noooo! This was a huge, four kilogram mother of an amethyst cluster. For one and a half hours we took turns carrying it up the beach. We passed ochre red cliffs, which at one point were broken by a small valley with bushes. On the top of the cliffs on either side of this ravine were two Aboriginal spirit people. As I walked towards them I received a very clear message that I was not permitted to enter. They were guarding a song line that ran through there. I didn't need to be told twice!

Just beyond this place three distinctly different rocks came together: red sand, white limestone with fossils of fish and shells, and jagged grey volcanic-looking rocks which hurt our feet to walk on. After a swim, sun bake and meditation we lugged the amethyst back to camp.

There was a full moon that night, so Susie put her rock out for a moon-bath by the edge of the sea. Intending to retrieve the amethyst in a couple of hours, we went back to the tent to meditate and do some balances for each other. We were so engrossed in what we were doing the hours flowed by unnoticed.

"Heavens, look at the time!" exclaimed Susie. Then nanoseconds later, "Holy shit! The crystal!"

Her baby was alone in the dark. After borrowing a flashlight from a stranger we set off to find the crystal cluster. The tide had gone out several hundred yards, leaving the boats stranded on the beach. The crystal was nowhere to be seen. It was too heavy to be dragged out by the tide, and we were convinced no one would steal it. Susie had left it lined up with a small metal dinghy, and we searched all around it to no avail. Deeply distressed, Susie and I went to bed.

Next morning she put up notices at the office and the restaurant:

> Lost: - one large amethyst cluster.
> Last seen by the sea, near the swimming pool.
> If you have found it please contact Susie at tent eight.

It was a little embarrassing explaining why the rock was left outside. The fishing blokes thought our moon-bathing rock was a great joke. We slunk off to have another search.

Mid-afternoon a day later there was a call at the door of our tent. There stood a man toting the crystal. Susie was overjoyed. It turned out that the metal dinghy landed on the crystal when the tide went out. When the tide came back in, the boat floated off and uncovered the amethyst. The owner of the boat remembered seeing Susie's sign and was able to return it.

One year later I was off to Monkey Mia again – this time to place a Galactic Wand. Diane suggested that she fly us up in a four-seater, single-engine Cessna 172, sharing the costs. I didn't need much convincing, and neither did Tony or Sheahara. The trip was much quicker by plane, but the down-sides to flying in a light aircraft were lack of storage space, which meant we were limited with the amount of food we could carry, and nausea from being bounced around in air pockets.

The plane hugged the coast almost all the way up, giving us spectacular panoramic views. Flying low enabled us to take in the stunning Zypdoorf cliffs that run for miles along the coast. We stopped to refuel and stretch our legs at Geraldton, then up and away again to Denham airport in Shark Bay.

Our arrival at the campsite was blessed by a group of huge glossy ravens nesting on the entrance posts.

Tony's eyes lit up. "Do you think that these ravens are the brothers that my crows at home were talking about?"

"Maybe," I said.

I figured that the army tent that I had hired with Susie the previous year would be perfect for us. It was open plan, roomy, had its own bathroom, slept six and had a basic kitchen. The mob loved it.

Our Scottish mate Kenneth arrived by car and dossed down with us for several nights. This broke up his drive to Broome to live with his new love and future wife, Angela.

We settled in, revelling in the relaxing holiday atmosphere. In the middle of the night Tony and I sat in the natural spring hot tub until we were prunes.

After the morning visit to the dolphins, the five of us packed drinks and snacks, then headed off along the coast to find a place to put the crystal. I sensed that the best place to start was near the song line I had found the previous year with Susie. We took our time, swimming, then walking and swimming some more. The conversation flowed effortlessly from one subject to another, as it does with good friends who love each other.

After a time Tony sped up, walking alone a couple of hundred yards ahead of the rest of us. He abruptly stopped and turned to face the gap in the cliffs where I had seen the Aboriginal spirits the previous year. I was very excited because I had deliberately not described it to anybody, wanting to see if they would find the same place as me.

We increased our pace to catch up with Tony. He stood silently staring at something; side-stepped and stood still again. Suddenly he dropped his bag, grabbed at his face and ran for the sea, diving in with clothes, sunglasses and all. When we arrived there he was still searching for his sunglasses on the sandy bottom.

Curious to know what had happened, we sat Tony down and waited for an explanation. Tony had spotted five ravens flying in the opposite direction to the way we were walking. He asked on the inside way if we needed to turn around. At that moment Tony spotted an Aboriginal spirit standing on the cliff pointing in the direction we were walking. This is the point at which he sped up his pace along the beach.

At the ravine he saw two spirits and Tony could feel the power of the song line. He turned to face the men and asked to enter the area. He received a resounding "No!" He stepped a few paces to the side and asked again, this time explaining that he came in peace and love with a wish to help heal this land.

He was answered by a huge swarm of flies so thick he was scooping them from his face in handfuls, precipitating his dash to the sea.

I shared with everyone that this was the same place that I had previously seen the Aboriginal guardians and felt the song line. We decided to walk to the promontory a little further ahead, where three distinctly different rocks merge. At the base of the cliff Tony found a large feather which looked like a sea eagle's.

We climbed the low cliff, then held hands forming a circle to meditate. We brought energy up from the Earth and became one with it. Then we drew energy down from the sky and the beings of Light in service to the planet. A strong breeze came up and a light rain began to fall; curiously, the only clouds in a perfect sky were the couple above us.

The flies became intolerable, crawling en masse into our ears, eyes and noses, making it extremely difficult to concentrate. I felt the presence of the three male Aboriginal spirit guardians. We dropped our hands and made space for the guardians to join our circle.

I explained that we wanted permission to heal the Ley Lines in the ocean and on the land in that area with the help of the extraterrestrials and the dolphins. As soon as I mentioned the dolphins they became much more receptive. I realized how much the dolphins were mediators between the Dreamtime guardians, the extraterrestrials and myself.

On the inside way the guardians granted us permission by rubbing ochre on our foreheads, cheeks and chins. We didn't get permission to enter the sacred site at the ravine, but we were granted permission to do our work and to put the crystal in the sea. After the ceremony the wind and rain stopped as abruptly as they had started.

Walking back home, Tony and I discussed the crow's message recorded months previously: "Look for my brothers and look for the fallen eagle." The ravens were obviously the brothers as they had alerted Tony to the presence of the spirit guardians.

"Do you think that the eagle's feather I found was the fallen eagle?"

"I think that's stretching it a bit, but it's a good sign," I replied.

*

The next morning at 6 am I sat down to meditate with the two Galactic Wands I had brought with me. The crystal to be placed at Monkey Mia was hot and pulsing in my left hand before the meditation had even begun, whereas the other crystal shard I had brought was cool in my right hand.

The blue light beings arrived, greeted me and I received the following messages:

- A fisherman will guide you to a spot to drop the crystal in the ocean. This will be directly out to sea from the red sand promontory.

- The crystal has already been energized and the appropriate programs in it activated during the night. (No wonder it was already hot!)

- Tony and you have to walk across the road to the cave where the three tribal guardians will be waiting for you. Meditate there and ask their permission to come back tonight.

- Tony and you need to massage each other's feet while you are at the cave. Then stand on your crystals and bring the energy down to activate more programs in the crystals.

- If possible, swim with the dolphins as they will energize and activate you. We will be pleased if you do this today as instructed.

After sharing my messages with Tony we set off to find a fisherman to take us out to sea. The locals weren't too keen about taking us out to swim in the ocean, as Tiger sharks were everywhere; and we were a bit reluctant to talk about crystals with them and explain why it was important. The only way we were going to get out to sea near the promontory was to pay for a trip to the pearl farm which was in the general direction of the red bluff.

The *Blue Lagoon* was skippered by the owner of the pearl farm. With us was a large group of Down's Syndrome adults. The many rows of pearling lines around the pontoon meant that we could not drop the crystal anywhere there. I received a message to drop the crystal on the way back from the pearl farm, so we settled down and enjoyed the tour.

On the return journey Tony felt drawn to talk to one of the volunteer women helping the Down's people. As we pulled away from the pontoon Tony chatted on the other side of the boat with the woman, Caroline, while I looked for the spot to place the crystal.

My jaw dropped with amazement as I scanned the coastline. From out to sea, the song-line area looked like a fallen eagle! The cliffs were the spread-out wings, and the bushes in the gap made the shape of an eagle's body and head.

I was instructed to drop the crystal in a line with the eagle's head. With my crystal-laden hand dangling nonchalantly over the side of the boat, I waited for the right moment. Seconds after I released it to the sea the skipper announced that we were just outside the pearl farming area.

Tony rushed over excitedly and started to tell me about the conversation he had with Caroline. Before the view was lost, I stopped him mid-sentence and pointed to the coast. "There's your fallen eagle, honey!"

Tony was so happy that the message he had received two months earlier was instrumental in helping us find the right place for the crystal. Now it was his turn to astound me. He continued where he had left off.

"I was chatting with Caroline about the open-hearted, loving qualities of the people in her care when she changed subjects and asked me if I was on holiday. I said, well sort of… not really…. it is difficult to explain.

"Then she said, 'You're here to heal the Ley lines, aren't you?' I was gob-smacked!"

He went on, "I explained to her that we were placing a Galactic Wand to heal a Ley Line. Caroline has a friend visiting from England who is here to place a crystal in Monkey Mia, too!

"Now get this," Tony said, nudging me for emphasis, "A psychic told her before she came up here that she would meet a man on a boat who was doing earth healing also. How about that!"

Right when I was dropping the crystal in the ocean, Tony was receiving this synchronistic confirmation. It dissolved any doubts about whether I was on the right track or not with what I was doing.

*

Just before sunset Tony and I walked to the small cave across the road from the Monkey Mia settlement. We climbed the hill above the cave, enjoying the magical isolation of Monkey Mia and the panoramic views. With our feet firmly nestled in the soft red sand, we called in the Aboriginal spirits. We asked permission to do a ceremony to bring more energy into the crystals. Again ochre was rubbed on our faces as a sign that it was okay to come back later that night.

Once night had fallen, Sheahara, Kenneth, Diane, Tony and I went to the hill above the cave with one flashlight to lead the way. Everyone was in good spirits, chatting and joking as we walked.

While Tony and I had been placing the crystal Sheahara had been teaching Diane Reiki Two. On the other side of the hill, Sheahara did the final initiation ceremony privately for Diane. On returning to the group, Sheahara channelled energy from Sanat Kumara for us. We each had a different experience, but the common denominator was a bright column of light coming down through the tops of our heads and into our bodies, accompanied by an increased intensity of energy.

We sat in the soft sand enjoying the clear, star-studded balmy night while Kenneth played his didgeridoo. He then gave us a sound healing by playing down the backs of our heads and spines. The music was beautiful, and the deep vibrations down my spine seemed to centre and ground me to the Earth. Next, I led a planetary healing meditation connecting us with the Earth and space intelligences, linking up with people all over the world of similar hearts and minds, forming a network of love and light across the planet.

Building on the contributions of thousands of other Light workers world-wide, we visualized the Ley Lines lining up with the electromagnetic grid in space around the Earth, creating harmony. With the help of the dolphins we activated the same lines in the seabed. I stood on my remaining crystal shard and Tony did the same with his as we all toned spontaneous sounds to activate the programs in the crystals.

After we completed the toning, something in the sky caught my attention. What initially appeared to be a star flashed red, green, blue and white. It moved rapidly across the sky, stopped, then did lightning-fast movements describing triangular shapes. By this time all five of us had noticed, and were mesmerized. The craft sped across the sky again and repeated the movements so fast it was a blur. Were they drawing upright pentagrams or a Star of David?

Just to make sure we had seen them, our space buddies did these manoeuvres in four different parts of the sky. Then within seconds the craft sped towards the eastern horizon and disappeared. What a show! Elated, we babbled about the gift of the UFO sighting all the way back to our tent.

Next morning Tony and I had one final laze in the hot tub before breakfast and a quick exit from Monkey Mia. With lots of heartfelt hugs and showers of kisses we said our good byes to Kenneth, wishing him well in his marriage to Angela. The flight home was smooth and wonderful. Shortly after our return to Perth, Sheahara flew home to Vancouver.

The Crystals Are Placed

In April Mary dropped in to tell me that the crystal I had given her custodianship of had found a home. She gave the crystal to Maxine, a Nyoongar from the southern coastal town of Denmark, who had placed it on land near the sea where she and friends had done a lot of healing.

Maxine was a Dreamtime artist, healer and storyteller. I telephoned Maxine to make sure that the crystal was properly placed and would not be found by anyone. Maxine and I never met, and I didn't find out the exact spot where the crystal was placed – there was no need. The job was done and it felt right.

*

I woke up from a busy night of dreaming about having to make decisions, and somehow the choices had to do with Aborigines. Later that morning Tony was drawn out to the backyard by a noisy bird. He called me to have a look. In the grand old olive tree next door was a flock of more than forty white-tailed black cockatoos. To Aborigines, both red-tailed and white-tailed black cockatoos are the spirits of their ancestors, and are messengers and harbingers of change and rain.

As we sat on the back step and watched, three flew close by across our yard, east to west. Then the rest of the flock flew by, a group or line at a time, four meters off the ground and a similar distance away from us.

One bird remaining behind as the others flew past was squawking quite persistently. I knew it had a message for me. When I tuned in I was told to go to Darwin in June/July and to HURRY UP!

Later that day I meditated to get more information:

• Tony's crystal, the Separation Crystal, must go to Darwin. It is a land rights crystal.

• The people of the Northern Territory are more connected to the land and its spirit than many others. This crystal will activate a line from Darwin through Uluru (Ayers Rock) to South Australia. South Australia is the most wounded, and the healing will travel along that line to S.A. [As my guides called it the Separation Crystal, I presumed that they were referring the "stolen generation" of Aboriginals. The nuclear testing carried out at Maralinga, South Australia, from 1956 to 1967 by the British, had probably disturbed the Song lines, causing this state's energy to be damaged].

• Be precise where it is put. It must go on a sacred site. Barbara will be a connecting link. (My friend Barbara lives in Adelaide).

• The threat from the sea will be altered because the energy and the consciousness of the people will be altered.

*

In another dream I was looking for a new home by the sea when a dolphin came right out of the water and flip-flopped up the beach towards me. I reached out to it and it gently kissed me on the hand before sliding back into the water. I walked a little further along the beach and a pod of six dolphins came out of the water to contact me.

I meditated to obtain more understanding of my dream. In the Senoi dream work tradition, I brought the dolphins from my dream into my meditation sacred space and asked the dolphins what they wanted. I went with the dolphins up the coast to Darwin and then to Arnhem Land. The dolphins communicated that the Separation Crystal needed to go to Arnhem Land, as this is the least damaged place in the Northern Territory.

I sought permission from the Aboriginal spirit elders to activate and place the crystal on a sacred site. I spent a long time explaining what it was for. They considered my request but gave no firm answer. We did several ceremonies together, which surprised me, because they were all men and I was a female.

Before she left for Vancouver, Sheahara had given me a large watery-green crystal ball. Someone in Canada had asked her to bring it to Australia and leave it in the heart of Australia.

This crystal was very cold to the touch, even after holding it for half an hour. The only person who could make it warm up was Amanda, Tony's daughter, who was visiting from England for a few weeks. The crystal ball was bathed in the sea on the full moon, and we did a cleansing meditation for it as well.

Wynelle did some dowsing for us and came up with some interesting information about the pale-green orb:

- It contains programs for the benefit of mankind.

- It has Lemurian recordings of ways of life and teachings before the great collapse.

There were also instructions:

- Place the crystal 10 inches below the ground in the Olgas (Kata Tjuta).

- Reconnect with the wisdom and knowledge of the old times.

- Link up with grid work in the Earth and above the Earth.

Sheahara was able to obtain information about the Galactic crystal shard designated for Adelaide. It was to be placed four miles east of the town centre, in nature. Dolphins and extraterrestrials from another galaxy would assist in linking the crystal to the Earth grid.

We knew that Tony's crystal had to go to the Northern Territory, and Sheahara's orb had to go to central Australia. I received a message that we needed to do a trip around Australia placing crystals in Adelaide, Queensland, the Northern Territory and central Australia.

Trusting our spiritual guidance implicitly, Tony and I planned a trip flying to Adelaide, Melbourne, Brisbane, Cairns, Darwin and Alice Springs. I was very excited about the trip because it meant I would be able to spend time in Adelaide with my son Craig, whom I missed greatly.

Armed with relatively little information, we flew to Adelaide. We stayed with an old friend, Barbara, as Craig had no room at his place. Craig came over to meet Tony for the first time and we talked for hours catching up. It was wonderful to see him and have some of his special hugs; my boys give the best hugs in the whole world.

I explained to Barbara that I needed to place a crystal four miles east of Adelaide, in nature, and asked if she had any clues as to where to start looking. My eyes lit up when Barb said, "Well, there's Eagle on the Hill, a hotel/restaurant in the Adelaide hills about that distance east of here."

"Fabulous," I said, "let's go!"

When we arrived at Eagle on the Hill and had a quick look around I said to Barb, "This is beautiful, but the crystal needs to be placed where no one will find it. Are there any national parks nearby?"

"Yep. This place backs onto a huge one – Cleland Conservation Park."

We went on a reconnaissance mission, saw the animals, such as koalas, then got a map of the park. As the crystal needed to be near water, I was drawn to Waterfall Gully. We decided to come back the next day and walk the waterfall trail.

The next morning Tony, Barbara and I walked the trail with the crystal in my backpack. We stopped to meditate at the waterfall numbered four on the map. It was a beautiful spot, but an Aboriginal male spirit appeared and pointed downstream, indicating that the spot for the crystal was further on. I was told that the place for the crystal was on the other side of the river.

At waterfall number three, perched above sheer rock on the other side of the river, was an Aboriginal spirit sitting cross-legged, singing and tapping his clapping sticks. He paused when our eyes met and pointed downstream. He then resumed his singing.

Waterfall two had low energy so we didn't investigate it.

The main waterfall was exquisite, with a huge old pine tree next to it, full of nature spirits and devas. It was not appropriate to place the crystal there as it was far too public. Castle Rock was above the main waterfall on the opposite side of the river, and I felt that somewhere there might be the crystal's home. Unfortunately, there wasn't enough time to climb it that day.

The next morning I meditated for more instructions:

- The crystal ball needs to be washed in the sea in each city that you visit before placing it in the Olgas. The orb is for reconnecting the damaged ones to the light.

- The Adelaide crystal has not been activated yet. Take Craig to the ocean today.

- You will see an Aboriginal spirit man where the crystal needs to be placed. Place the crystal near water.

- Be on your own for a while today to meditate. Allow everything today to play itself out. Resist the need to fix anything.

- You are being guided to a particular place today. Stay open.

- Hug a tree and connect your energy with the tree and into the earth. Connect with the dolphin energy today.

After Craig finished work we went to North Glenelg Beach where the Patawalunga River comes to the sea. Bracing ourselves against the cold we sat facing the ocean and the setting sun. Craig used Tony's Tibetan singing bowl while we all toned. I showed Craig how to rub the bowl with its wooden stick clockwise to call in the Light beings (angels), then to

107

sound anticlockwise as we asked the Light beings to cleanse us and the surrounding area. The third part of this process was to ring the bowl clockwise again as Archangel Michael placed an electric blue field of protection around us and Saint Germain bathed us in the violet flame of purification.

Craig continued to sound the bowl while Tony and I meditated, connecting with the dolphins and the Aborigines in Cleland Park. The Aborigines were having a jubilant corroboree on the top of Castle Rock above the big waterfall. This convinced me that this was where the crystal needed to go.

On the inside way, a whale guided me out to sea where there was an underwater energy centre pulsating with an erratic light. The energy vortex was malfunctioning and emitting disharmonious energy. The whale asked me to remove the faulty crystal. As I removed it I could see that it was black. The whale gave me a shining clear quartz, which I placed in the hole, which was sealed and activated with a golden orb from my solar plexus. I then channelled light down through my crown chakra and out my heart chakra to the dark crystal, causing it to turn to dust.

Once the meditation was complete Tony bathed Sheahara's green crystal orb in the sea seven times.

The next day Tony and I climbed up Castle Rock. We could see the city and the sea on two sides. No one else was there except a black crow, which looked at us, then flew further up the rocks over our heads. This spot was where I had seen the Aboriginal spirits having a corroboree in my meditation at the beach.

As this was where a lot of tourists came, we climbed higher in the direction that the crow had flown. Above us and slightly to the left we found a beautiful outcrop of rocks with a sheer drop below it. We sat and meditated, connecting the crystal in my hand with the Aboriginal, extraterrestrial and dolphin energies and the reactivated crystal in the sea bed. Transmuting into crows we flew all over South Australia. The northern and western areas were covered in a grey cloud, which we cleared.

I was instructed to place the crystal due south and three degrees up from horizontal. Tony found the perfect spot, but it was pretty hair-raising watching him place it. The hotel near where we had sat on the beach was an easy landmark to detect on the horizon. So in divine right order once again, the crystal found its home, pointing towards the sea in the exact direction of the reactivated crystal in the seabed!

After fond farewells with Barbara and Craig we flew to Melbourne to visit Tony's children. In Melbourne and Brisbane, I conducted Kinesiology workshops to help pay for the trip.

*

When we were in Cairns I meditated for more instructions. "The Queensland crystal needs to go to an island north of Cairns. You will place the crystal today. You need to get permission on the inside way when you find the place. Allow the eagle to guide you. Borrow Craig's car and go north."

Following this guidance, Tony and I borrowed a car from our hosts, Craig and Rae-Lee. We went to Mosman and the Daintree forest. It was magical exploring the lush tropical walk trails alongside roaring rivers canopied by enormous ancient trees. We meditated by the river, allowing the damp undergrowth to cool us.

Port Douglas felt very commercial and pretentious after our short stint in the bush. We looked at Double Island and

Haycock Island but couldn't nut out a way to get there. All those boat fares were way outside our budget for the trip. The picturesque scenery along the coast couldn't dissolve my frustration. I was supposed to place the crystal, and I had failed to find the spot.

The next day Tony and I climbed Pyramid Mountain. It was an enjoyable climb, but we were disheartened that we had still not found the place for the crystal. My guidance was still telling me that the crystal was meant for an island near Cairns, for the stability of the Earth and the Great Barrier Reef.

We drove to the Yarrabah Aboriginal Community to look at Rocky Island. The road there was steep and winding, causing the labouring old car to ping and belch smoke. The Aboriginal community was a mixed bag energetically, with a good school and community hall but many of the homes looking sad and unloved. This wasn't the place.

As we left the area Tony spotted an eagle overhead so we pulled over and got out of the car. The eagle spiralled upwards on an air current, flew in the direction of Cairns, then out to sea.

The day before we left Cairns I went on my own to Green Island. I received no messages about the crystal. The snorkelling there was excellent – electric-blue starfish, giant clams, vibrant coral and myriads of fish in psychedelic colours. While I was sun-baking on the beach a sea eagle dive-bombed into the water and came out with a fish.

In spite of all this beauty I was annoyed with myself. Yes, we had seen eagles, but not one place we had gone to felt right to leave the crystal in, and I wasn't going to leave it just anywhere in the vicinity. I wasn't sure whether my guidance was wrong, or whether I just wasn't reading the signs. Were my guides testing me? I had no answers. The only thing I knew was that the Queensland crystal was not going to be placed on this trip.

On writing this story, years later, it is now obvious why I didn't find a home for the crystal then. At no time during that trip in Queensland did I see an Aboriginal spirit! Every time I have done Earth healing work in Australia, the Aboriginal spirit elders have shown themselves to me, given permission on the inside way and pointed to where they wanted the crystals to go. In fact, the only time I see them is when there is work to be done.

The elders evidently did not want the crystal to go where my guides had said. Unfortunately, at the time I felt that I had somehow failed or fallen short of what was asked of me.

On 22 August we arrived in Darwin and stayed the night in a pokey air-conditioned dog-box. The setback in Cairns had dampened our confidence, causing some confusion as to what to do next. The Separation Crystal couldn't be placed in Arnhem Land because we didn't have a permit, and permits were not granted quickly or too freely.

Finally we decided to hire a bubble car and drive to Kakadu National Park. Kakadu abuts onto Arnhem Land, so it would be the next best place. Tony did all the driving, which suited me fine.

We camped the first night at Merl Bush Camp, where there were very clean shower and toilet facilities. The mosquitoes ate us alive as we slept fitfully in the car. The next morning we played tourist. The rock art at Ubirr was fascinating, and the lookout treated us to breathtaking views that made both of us very emotional. This area had a special soft energy to it, which made me feel welcome and at home.

The Gallery was particularly inviting. I imagined a large mob of Aborigines sheltering there during the wet season, telling stories and teaching the youngsters. We went on the mangrove rainforest walk and saw our first crocodile on the opposite bank. That night I dreamed of Aboriginal Spirit elders singing and playing didgeridoos around me. I woke up still seeing them and feeling their presence strongly around the car.

If you ever want to treat yourself to wonderful countryside, go to Kakadu. It is truly magnificent! We went on a pleasant and interesting cruise up the East Alligator River while the Guluyambi Aboriginal guides talked to us about their land, cultural heritage and way of life. They were good-humoured and easygoing. "One side of the river is Kakadu National Park and the other side is Arnhem Land," one of the guides informed us as we headed upstream.

Our third night at Kakadu was at Muirella Park and was very restful. After breakfast we walked three kilometres in the scorching heat to Gubara Waterhole in the hope of a refreshing swim. Fat chance! We found a few stagnant pools only calf deep. The three-kilometre walk back to the car brought us to a slow simmer. Still not getting the hint, we braved a four-kilometre walk to Nanguluwir Art Site. Thoroughly fricasseed with sunstroke by then, we opted to skip the Nowranagie Art Site and go straight to the cool of the Warradjan Aboriginal Cultural Centre.

We were gradually working our way down through the Park from the coast – inland. Neither Tony nor I had any clear messages regarding the crystal and were concerned that we would be out of the Park before finding a home for it. I meditated and received a vision of a tall waterfall with water cascading down a flat, vertical rocky face into a deep pool. As it was the dry season we didn't expect to find any running waterfalls in Kakadu.

All the main roads in the park were sealed. When we looked for the nearest waterfall, which was Gunlom, we noted that the road in was gravel. The hire car was new and air-conditioned, so we trusted that the corrugations and dust from the road wouldn't bother us too much. The dirt road turned out to be pretty well-maintained and we arrived safely at Gunlom at dusk. After dinner and a shower we turned in for the night.

Quite frankly, after the heat and let-down of the previous day we weren't sure there would even be any water at Gunlom "swimming hole". I couldn't believe my ears the next morning when we came close to the pool – the sound of running water!

You could have blown me over with a feather. There was the exact waterfall and pool from my meditation! The pool was large and looked very deep. A steady stream of water flowed from a great height down a sheer rock face. Without question, we had found the place for the crystal.

Climbing to the top of the falls we discovered a series of pools and waterfalls above the main one. In the third pool, high above the original, was a large rocky outcrop shaped like a snake's head.

"Wow! This is the Rainbow Serpent in person!" I said excitedly.

We climbed near the snake's head and meditated. Once again I activated an energy centre in the seabed with the guidance of the dolphins. The crystal was placed pointing northwest towards Darwin and the islands off the coast. This was definitely a special water place. An enormous frog-shaped rock also stood guard over the crystal.

Our task complete, we celebrated by swimming and exploring this paradise for hours. To our delight we discovered that there were lots of waterfalls and swimming holes outside Kakadu. Our trip back to Darwin was punctuated by refreshing swims at Florence Falls, Tolmer Falls and Wangi.

*

My guides told me it was time to activate the green crystal ball that was to be placed at the Olgas.

Tony's hands held the top of the ball while mine cradled the bottom. We toned like this for five minutes, allowing energy to flow through us to activate the old knowledge contained in the crystal and merge it with present consciousness. The guides said the crystal was to be placed ten inches underground, just as Wynelle had dowsed, in the shadow of three rounded hills/rocks. They telepathically gave me a picture of what this place looked like.

Darwin airport was overflowing with hundreds of army personnel now that Kangaroo '95 was over. Australia, New Zealand, Indonesia and the USA had been involved in war games in the Northern Territory. We flew to Alice Springs, then on to Ayers Rock. The Outback Pioneer Hotel was a luxury after all the roughing it in the car. A day off recuperating and being totally indulgent was just what the doctor ordered.

The little Mira we hired took us to Uluru (Ayers Rock). The cultural centre was very interesting, as were the Anangu Aborigines talking about their culture, spinning hair and food gathering. The male tourists were invited to have a go at throwing a spear at a cardboard emu. Tony threw the spear and missed. Suddenly he felt nauseous and his brain felt as if it moved in his head, causing it to hurt. Instead of walking around the base of Uluru, we drove back to the hotel where Tony flopped on the bed and immediately fell asleep. After

114

Tony had rested, he still felt ill and out of sorts so I did a Kinesiology balance for him. This led to a past life regression to the Uluru area 6324BC.

In that life Tony was an old Aboriginal man in his forties or fifties. He had a son about twenty years old, who went to a sacred site that was taboo for him. The son was not allowed on that site until his father (Tony) had passed away. Going on the site before his time was against tribal law.

Tony and the men of his tribe chased the son for five days. He was good at covering his tracks but he was eventually caught and brought back to camp. The men beat the son with sticks, and Tony had to spear him, but he couldn't bring himself to spear his son. He kept aiming for his legs and missing. The tribal men ended up killing Tony and his son with clubs. The Rainbow Serpent came for their spirits and they rested inside the rocks.

Missing the cardboard emu with the spear at Uluru had triggered the distressing memory of the lifetime in that area. Once the healing was complete Tony's health and energy returned.

Next morning I woke up with a vision of large rocks near an archway of rock, and a conviction that this vision was connected to placing the crystal orb.

Tony and I drove to Kata Tjuta (Olgas) and did the Valley of the Winds walk. It is a very female place with rocks shaped like vaginas and vulvas everywhere. We found three domed rocks creating shade, just as my guides had shown me. The energy in this spot was very gentle, grounding and nurturing.

As the place was rocky, we headed up a gully off the main track to find a place with soil. Before us was a low rock arch, and I knew we were going to find the spot on the other side. We found some shade from the intense heat of the sun, and toned while we both held the crystal. Out loud I asked the spirit guardians of that place for permission to leave the crystal there. I saw an Aboriginal woman with big breasts and white markings painted on her body and face. She put ochre and paint on me and stood in the gap of a hollowed-out tree, pointing to the base of the tree.

Two sparring Aboriginal men appeared and challenged each other. They danced around and merged into one calm older man who stood next to the woman, now suckling a baby.

We went to the hollowed-out tree. Tony dug down ten inches, put the crystal in and covered it with sand, leaves and rocks. He felt very emotional: joy tinged with sadness. We then went for a quiet, reflective walk in the gorge.

On returning to Perth we settled back into our work routine.

*

In September '95 Maggie and Bev shared their crystal placing story in the following letter:

> *Dear Patti,*
>
> *We have just returned from Cape Leveque and I'm happy to report that the crystal has been placed.*
>
> *We hired a small 4WD in Broome and negotiated the 270 kilometres of narrow track fraught with deep sand rifts. It wasn't long before we discovered that a larger vehicle would have been more suitable.*
>
> *Cape Leveque was everything we dreamed. We rented a fronded hut right on the ocean, from the local community.*

It was open on two sides, with a BBQ in one corner and a cold water shower on a slab of concrete in the other. The only furnishing a picnic table.

Right away we were at peace and drank in the splendour of the place. We unrolled our swags on the sand and set the esky on the table.

Maggie unpacked the crystal wrapped in clothes in her backpack.

"What now?" we wondered.

We were engrossed in boiling the billy and making sandwiches for lunch when three Aboriginal men appeared.

"Quick, quick, come see,," they invited, smiling and waving their arms.

We followed, intrigued.

"Look, look." We looked to where they were pointing out to sea.

There were two or three whales playing with their calves; blowing them in the air, diving and leaping like children at play. We joined the men in the delight of the spectacle that went on for an hour or more.

Afterwards over a pot of tea the men told us that they had never seen whales behave like that before. We were all thrilled to have witnessed it. The men, members of the Bardie community from further around the headland, invited us to visit them the next day.

Later that evening Maggie was looking at the rocky cliff above where the whales had been.

"I think that is the place." She said "Early tomorrow we'll climb up there and see."

117

We knew that not only did we have to seek guidance as to where to place the crystal; it needed to be safe from cyclones and the high tides that the area was noted for.

At first light we went in search of a resting-place for the crystal. The energy felt right, and as we climbed higher we came upon a deep crack in the rock. Maggie was sure this was the place. We sat and meditated and sent Reiki. Then we placed the crystal in the crack and placed other stones on top.

We laughed to think that the whales were trying to get our attention and we were too busy making lunch to notice. So the locals had to come and point them out to us.

We had a magical few days there. The Bardie people welcomed us into their community with such open hearts that I felt humbled. We were taken to meet every member of the community and given a huge chunk of turtle meat that fed us for three days.

One of the men we had first met and an elder of the community insisted on taking us out to see Sunday Island. We waded out to a dinghy through crocodile-infested mangrove swamps. We were very nervous, with eyes looking everywhere for crocs, much to the men's delight.

Then came the serious business of negotiating treacherous seas with large whirlpools caused by the gigantic tides. The young man steered, never taking his eyes off the subtle finger gestures of guidance from the elder. We felt perfectly safe and enjoyed the trip past many small islands to our destination.

So the crystal has landed in a very special place, inhabited by some very extraordinary people. The experience will stay with us forever and we feel honoured to have placed it. We're looking forward to seeing you soon, till then...

Much Love, Maggie and Bev

*

In October '95 Kenneth wrote me a lovely long letter saying that he and Angela had placed their crystal. Here are the best bits:

Hi Patty and Tony!!

Wow! Incredible things have been happening. Angie's pregnant (10 weeks), we both feel like it is a girl. When she conceived (vaguely around this time) we saw three dolphins playing in the water in front of the house for three hours. Next day we hired a dinghy and tried to find them. We did. They played with us for half an hour, swimming belly up under the boat, surfacing next to us and eyeing us up. They were really interested in the didgeridoo I was playing out the side of the boat!

Anyway Angie was particularly moved by all this and couldn't get the image of dolphins out of her mind. A week later she is having continuous dreams of dolphins bringing a little girl to her and protecting them both. Then whammo! She's pregnant!!

Now on to the crystal: I started to get worried that my crystal had switched off or gone to sleep or something because I felt no real push or prod from it to say, "Let's go!"

Then I had a disaster dream a month ago. I dreamed of a huge tidal wave coming over the house around 2.30 in the afternoon. I was calm and accepting of this inevitable wave.

Recently I had a different disaster dream. I was sitting on the rocks near the ocean, in front of the house, when I noticed an orange glow along the northwest horizon out at sea. A huge dark cloud was coming from it. I somehow knew it was a massive oceanic volcano erupting!

A shock blast of hot wind tore across the land and flattened everything. The origin of the glow was too far away and

119

below the horizon to see. I saw huge ships sinking out to sea. Then the fiery glow was getting brighter. Lava flows were somehow evaporating the ocean and heading towards the land. Again I was calm and accepting.

This dream really made an impression on me and then a friend, who had gone to a channelling night, told me of how whales and dolphins are setting up a "GRID" to alleviate a huge natural disaster. I started to feel that time was running out

Last week Angie and I drove 1100 km to Keep River National Park. The place that was on the map you gave me with the crystal. I'd looked often at the cave paintings in the photos and felt attracted to one in particular.

I had given Kenneth photos of Aboriginal art and a map of Keep River National Park. Wynelle had dowsed that his crystal had to go there.

As we drove up there I was riddled with doubts. I had meditated and Reiki'd the situation to gain insight as to where the correct spot was but received no answers! I pleaded with the universe to help guide me.

Angie was driving at night and ran over a huge snake moving sinuously across the road. She couldn't get the image of the snake out of her head. Then she saw in her mind a cave painting of a huge brown snake.

"The crystal has to go to the serpent," she said.

Now I felt this was true since in one of the pictures of the rock paintings there was a large Rainbow Serpent.

Anyway we got there, saw the spot and knew it was right. As I placed the crystal a huge wind blew up and went through me like an incredible electric charge. Cicadas started chirping and the Aboriginal Spirit Bird called out. Angie heard this too.

The site was Cockatoo Dreaming of the Mirriwung people and was actually once the ocean floor millions of years ago. I placed the crystal into rock pointing in a northerly direction.

From where the crystal is, the only feature in a Northerly direction is a place called "Spirit Hills" and then on to the coast at Joseph Bonaparte Gulf.

Driving home to Broome, I received an incredible vision of tribal elders chanting around the hole, withdrawing the crystal, and the serpent painting coming alive! A huge serpent's head hovered menacingly in front of them. "Holding the space", the elders threw the crystal down its throat.

I followed the serpent as it spun around and flew into the rock hole. I hung onto its neck and we burrowed deep into the Earth's mantle. We headed upwards, finally exploding out of a hole which was the plug of an erupting volcano!

I floated thousands of feet into the air as the Rainbow Serpent, on colliding with the ground, split into hundreds of serpents. They shot off in all directions like electrical currents in a circuit board, across grey sand in a flat primeval landscape. As they travelled, they formed rivers, gorges, mountains and all natural features.

I then fell to Earth in flames like a shooting star. I ran across the grey sand until I saw an intense ball of white light twenty foot across, hovering just above the ground. A voice thanked me for delivering the crystal and said that I had done well! Then I saw my Aboriginal elder friend who smiled like a Cheshire cat (first time he had looked that happy).

Anyway that's what happened. Whacky stuff, eh? Let us know what you guys know about these crystals, their purpose, whose involved etc., as I am really keen to know what the hell I've been involved in!

Take care you guys and keep in touch!

Love, Kenneth and Angie x x

121

*

In February 1996 Diane received a message in meditation to go to Geraldton and that she would be told what to do. Every day for two months she asked her guides about the trip to Geraldton.

"Trust! You need to go," was the continual frustrating reply. Finally she was instructed to "Go in two weeks' time by car with Roz, Patti and Tony. Don't fly because you will need the car."

Tony couldn't come because of work commitments and Penny coming to stay. I suggested that we might need to do crystal and Ley Line healing. After checking with her guides Diane was instructed to get her Galactic Wand from Auntie, who had been caretaking it for a while, and take it to Geraldton.

On 30th April Diane, Roz and I drove up towards Geraldton in Diane's Land Rover. On the way we called in to Dongara to visit family for the morning and have lunch in the Dongara Café. While we were eating, I spotted Max walking into the cafe. I recognized him from when he had filmed kids on the Supercamp. At that time Max was doing filming for the 11am Australia TV show.

Diane never fails to surprise me. She just outright asks this virtual stranger where we should place the crystal! Max was pretty flummoxed by the question but when he regained his composure he said he thought Dongara or Kalbarri would be better places as they had better energy.

Bold as brass Diane then asked Max if he would film the Royal Flying Doctor Air Race that she and her mate Gina flew in each year. She assured him it was loads of fun and a great fund-raiser for the Flying Doctor. He said yes! Max left and we headed off to the beach at Dongara to meditate. Roz got a message about a church and the colour red.

I had an image of the river meeting the sea. I was told that there were three places that we had to go to – one being the beach where we were. Also I was told to go with what Diane was instructed to do.

The message Diane received was that the crystal was to be placed in Dongara and that I would find the place. I told Diane that this was her crystal and that she had to meditate again to get the details herself, follow her guidance, and trust it, not me.

She was instructed that the crystal had to be at the beach and that we should sleep at the Backpackers' tonight. (Roz wasn't too happy about that as she has a Princess and the Pea complex. Four star accommodation or above for her – none of this roughing it!). We needed to find the place for the crystal tonight, then activate and place it the next morning.

Following Roz's indicators, we drove towards the red hill and turned left into Church Street. We followed Church Street to the end and climbed a lookout hill. There below was a river meeting the sea and the red-roofed, four-star accommodation Roz had been putting out for. We dropped our luggage in a villa overlooking the ocean, then went in search of the spot for the crystal.

We followed a trail of red plastic pieces of rubbish strewn along the beach to the mouth of the river. Even the water was red from the sunset. Six birds flew from the beach at the river mouth to red weeds on the brackish riverbank. Diane followed them and found a good hiding place for her crystal amongst the rocks and red weeds.

At five thirty in the morning I woke up to a room filled with light, although the curtains were drawn, the light was off and it was dark outside. Before daylight Diane and I hauled Roz out of bed and we walked by flashlight to the mouth of the river. We sat in the sand facing the ocean, positioned between two rocks out to sea from the river mouth. Using my Tibetan singing bowl I did the same cleansing and protecting ritual that Craig had done in Adelaide, while we all toned. On the inside way I followed some whales out to sea from Dongara. They took me deep, deep, deep down into a chasm, deeper than I had been before. I pulled on the metal handle of a trap door in the floor bed that the whales led me to. Beneath the trap door was a cluster of crystals, which I activated.

I was then led to a glowing, active crystal cluster in the ocean out from Geraldton. I was incredulous when I was instructed to smash it. The crystals held negative old patterns. A few yards further out to sea from the original, a new crystal cluster was activated to bring through new patterns of consciousness.

At Kalbarri, whales and a pod of dolphins were frolicking around a third crystal cluster. These three centres in the ocean floor formed a triangle pointing away from the coast. I was shown an image of three centres on the land in each town forming a triangle pointing away from the coast.

After the activation we walked to the spot that Diane had chosen on the edge of the river. Four black swans and a white heron were quietly feeding nearby on the estuary. We held hands and connected the energies of the six sites (three in the ocean and three on land) with the earth energies. Via Roz we sent the pink ray of love from our hearts to all of creation. Diane then hid the crystal shard.

124

Diane said disappointedly, "You know the only thing that is missing is the kookaburra! I was told that a kookaburra would be with me and guide me."

I said practically, "You won't find a kookaburra around here."

As we turned to walk away we heard a kookaburra laughing! In unison, with mouths agape, we turned back to the river. There was only the white heron wading in the water. The heron flew off in front of us repeating its call. It was the best kookaburra impersonation I had ever heard! We chortled at Diane's kookaburra confirmation via a heron.

Archangel Michael

Tony and I were looking for a new place to rent. Every time that we felt we had the right place, the deal fell through for one reason or another. Just as we were despairing of finding a new house, the Love Bunny returned to Perth. Sheahara wove her special brand of magic again. Tony and I both had Reiki haircuts to help find the right home for us.

A week later we were given information about home loans that only required a one-thousand dollar deposit! We hadn't thought of buying a home. Within one month we had bought a lovely home in Mt Nasura, five minutes' drive from Diane's home. My son Adam and some of his mates took over the rental of the house we had all shared, marking a new stage in his life as an adult.

Every morning at 6 am, Tony, Diane and I would go for a brisk walk in the bush. It was a time when we would share our messages from meditations and mull over the significance of our dreams, or just let off steam over family or work problems. I cherished this time we had together, sharing, laughing and encouraging each other. When necessary, we would be very honest and "call" each other on limiting behaviour, projections or denials, about certain people or situations.

We alternated between two walks. The walk near our house was very hilly, with wonderful views over the city to the coast. It was a great walk for getting the heart rate up and provoking the odd puff, pant and whinge. The track behind Diane's house was on a ridge in State forest. It was flatter, but a joy because of the wildflowers, trees and wildlife. Kangaroos, emus, feral goats and bobtail goannas were often seen, which enthralled Congee, Diane's overweight dog, who would tear off in vain attempts to bail them up. At these times, the peace and tranquillity of the bush would be temporarily shattered by Diane hollering at the top of her lungs for Congee to come back.

Kookaburras are Diane's totem. She laughs loudly all the time, so the kookaburras mirror her infectious, bubbly and uplifting personality. It is impossible to be depressed when Diane is around. Diane's trademark is YAHOO!!!! She'll walk into any room or gathering anywhere and announce her arrival by yelling "Yahoo!" at the top of her voice, then dissolve into peels of infectious laughter. Her thick untameable gypsy hair and wild uninhibited manner add to the effect.

Often when spirit wanted to communicate with Diane and was having trouble getting her attention, kookaburras would fly into her bedroom window with a crash. They would then peck on the window until she tuned in for the message. They would even visit her in the wee small hours of the night.

We regularly saw white tailed and red tailed black cockatoos on our walks. The red tail feather of the female cockatoo is extra special to me because it has the colours of the Aboriginal flag in it. Often when we talked about significant things, black cockatoos would fly into the trees next to us and start squawking loudly. (The elders were always nearby keeping an eye on us.)

127

On these walks, if Diane shared something important about herself, the kookaburras would start laughing as if to lend weight to what she was saying. This in turn made us laugh at the synchronicity of it all.

No matter which walk we went on, halfway around we would stop and meditate. At the end of June 1996 we meditated on our special overhanging rock with a stunning view to the east, over the valley and hills of the forest. After this particular meditation Tony shared what had happened for him. Archangel Michael appeared to him, athletic and handsome. He was naked to the waist with flowing robes from his hips to his ankles. Michael was bent over, resting his chin on the hilt of his huge sword, the tip of which was in the ground. Tony asked him why he was dressed differently to the Catholic picture he had of him. He said that it was a *Roman* Catholic picture, so they had him dressed in the garb of a Roman soldier.

Following this informal chat, Tony said what we had both often affirmed in meditation:

"I surrender my will to Divine Will, in peace, love and light." Then Tony said, "I am now ready to take my next spiritual step."

Archangel Michael smiled quietly to himself as he looked Tony in the eye, stood up, grasped his sword in two hands and gently speared Tony in the abdomen just below his right ribs.

Tony gasped with surprise at this, looked down and saw black, inky smoke oozing from the wound as the sword was removed. He looked incredulously at Michael and asked why he had done it.

"You have some darkness in there that needs some light shed on it" was his reply. What a powerful meditation!

By the time we got back home, Tony's stomach and liver areas were in pain. The next morning he woke up jaundiced. His eyes, skin and nails were very yellow and his urine was red with what we thought was blood. I thought it was hepatitis.

His blood tests came back clear of any type of hepatitis. Tony was in pain, tired and unable to eat much. If he ate, he vomited it back up.

An ultrasound was taken which showed a possible blockage or growth. My heart sank. I knew instinctively that something was seriously wrong. Further scans, blood tests and an endoscopy were inconclusive. The only way to be sure was to open him up.

"Oh shit!" I thought to myself.

The weekend before Tony went into hospital, we attended Victor Barron's Guardian Angel workshop. We did an exercise in pairs, where your guardian angel heals your partner. I was paired with Tony. My angel removed a seven-year-old version of Tony from his liver area and put the child on my knee to cuddle, while the angel worked etherically on Tony. Tony's dead father, whom he had never been allowed to meet, came to me and gently and lovingly took the seven-year-old Tony with him to the spirit world. This meditation confirmed for me that Tony's illness was in part due to unresolved pain and abandonment from childhood.

In the lunch break, Victor Barron did a shamanic healing for Tony. Victor told Tony that he definitely did not have cancer. Several friends assured me that Tony did not have anything serious. I kept my mouth shut because my intuition was telling me otherwise. I prayed that I was wrong.

Tony and I went to the hospital chapel before his operation

129

to pray. As we were leaving, the resident chaplain introduced himself.

"Hello, my name is Michael. If you need me for anything, I am always here to help." Tony and I laughed.

"Of course your name is Michael! What other name would you have?" I said cryptically to the priest. We left the chapel reassured that we were being looked after by the boys upstairs.

While Tony was undergoing surgery, my stalwart friends, Bev and Maggie, came with me to the hospital chapel to send Reiki to Tony and meditate. In my meditation, Archangel Michael came to me and said, "Patti, Tony has cancer. He is going to die and there is nothing you can do about it. You will not be able to heal him. We repeat, you will *not* be able to heal him! He is needed elsewhere. Your job is to help him to be as complete as possible before he goes. I am telling you now so that you don't feel that you have failed him when he dies."

I had spent all of my life searching for a partner with whom I was compatible on all levels, bringing out the best in each other. I had finally found my match in Tony. We had been idyllically happy for eighteen months. Each day we counted our blessings and expressed our gratitude for being together. Now my darling man was being taken from me! I came out of the meditation fighting back the tears.

Maggie and Bev looked at me expectantly and asked me what I had received in my meditation.

Using the hot potato method, I said, "What did you get?"

Maggie threw the potato back in a gentle, steady voice, "Honey, what did you get?"

130

I told them about Michael, and that Tony had cancer. I left out the bit about him dying because I didn't want to speak it into existence. Maggie agreed that she thought he had cancer too. I thanked God that I had one friend who would be honest with me while everyone else was in a Pollyanna, optimistic mode. From that moment Maggie became my confidante, the one I could be frank with and share with what I really felt.

I am blessed with the number of human angels I have supporting me. Bev lives in the country four hours' drive away, yet she drove all the way up to Perth just to be with us at this trying time.

Maggie and Bev left, and in tag–team style my niece Katie took over for them. Katie waited with me. Tony had left strict instructions for me to be told the results before he came out of the anaesthetic. The previous tests had been harrowing because of endless waiting with nurses who knew the results but were legally unable to tell me.

Five agonizing hours later, a doctor finally confirmed that Tony had gall bladder cancer. The tumour was the size of an apple and was inoperable because it was lying over all of the main arteries and veins. It was pressing on the bile duct, which is why he was yellow and had reddish-brown urine. The cancer was also enclosing the duodenum, so food couldn't pass from the stomach into the small intestine. This explained the vomiting. There were secondary cancers in his abdomen.

The surgeon did bypass surgery to create a new pathway for the bile, and reattached the small intestine higher up on the stomach. This would buy Tony some time and allow him to eat again.

Poor Katie! As a nurse she knew the seriousness of the situation. She struggled valiantly to find some encouraging words to say.

I told Tony everything, as promised, as soon as he came out of the anaesthetic. Tony gazed out the window as he absorbed the news. "Look at that!" he cried excitedly, as he pointed to the sky. There was a large brown eagle flying high above the hospital. This was in a built-up area of Fremantle and the last place we would expect to see one.

My beautiful man was very sick. He vomited and vomited old black blood. Black blood flowed from the other end too. He was in a lot of pain with the vomiting because he had an arched incision scar all along under his rib cage from one side to the other. I felt so helpless, and he was being so brave.

He became very weak, his energy dropping through the floor. There was a dark, still energy around him. My guides told me he was deciding whether to die now or stay longer. Sweet Jesus, I wasn't ready for that.

The doctor recommended a blood transfusion as Tony had lost so much blood. I could see Tony momentarily toy with the idea of refusing the transfusion; then he agreed to have it. Within twenty-four hours, his energy picked up and I knew he had decided to stay alive a bit longer.

Once when Tony required an enema I left the ward to get some refreshments. On my return I found the nurse laughing and shaking her head as she exited the room. In response to my inquiring look Tony explained. After the nurse had performed her duties on his rear end Tony had looked over his shoulder, batted his eyelashes and coyly asked, "Does this mean that we are engaged now?" He was so buoyant in the face of adversity, always having a smile and joke readily accessible.

I made up a spray bottle of Rescue Remedy and other flower essences and sprayed the room regularly. I also gave him flower essences in the mouth. My aroma therapist friend, Terrie, lent us a nebulizer which I had going for several hours each day. The steam vapours carried the perfume of rose otto, sandalwood and frankincense throughout the room and down the hall. Nurses and doctors would pop into the room to find out where the lovely smell was coming from, or just to have a quick olfactory fix. After several days the nurses commented that the aromatherapy was having a positive effect on the whole hospital floor and particularly on the staff!

When Tony could eat and drink normally again, he was allowed home.

In the midst of all this was Tony's son Sebastian's 21st birthday. Paul flew to Melbourne with the air ticket that Tony was too ill to use. With him he carried the antique wine glasses and Taylor's Vintage Port Reserve 1967 which were Tony's presents to Sebastian. The most precious present had already been faxed – a poem for Sebastian, written by Tony, which was read out at the birthday party. He was so disappointed that he could not be there to give the customary speech for his much loved son.

Tony's illness brought his family much closer together, causing the usual petty squabbles and sibling rivalries to be forgotten.

Tony's tummy stuck out whenever he sat up or stood up. The scar healed cleanly, but he had to walk around holding his stomach. Finally after two months of our mentioning the problem, the doctor diagnosed an operational hernia. All the vomiting just after the operation had opened up the incision line. The skin had healed, but the muscles were apart, and his guts were literally hanging out. Luckily, the opening was so large it wasn't pinching anything. So into hospital again, to stitch Tony up. More pain. Tony loved me to rub his feet with peppermint lotion to take his mind off everything. We also became very good at card games.

Two significant people came to see Tony when he was in hospital the first time. One was a Buddhist monk who had once had cancer of the bladder. His wife left him, and he did the whole recovery on his own. Eight years later, he had a clean bill of health and considered himself cured. The other was a friend of mine who was in remission from brain tumours. They were both inspirations to Tony. They gave him the strength to live and overcome the cancer. It meant much more to Tony to hear first-hand stories of people who had gone through the same ordeal as he, and won. However, he was not interested in attending any cancer support groups.

The responsibility of knowing that Tony would die weighed heavily on me over the following months. I kept asking myself, "Am I just being negative?" I believed that you could be on death's door and still be restored to full health. With the right attitude, life style, diet, healing techniques and spiritual practices, a full recovery was possible. I had met Ian Gawler at a talk years before, and he was an inspirational, living testament to this. There was an exhausting tug of war going on within me. On the one hand was my knowledge that miraculous healing was possible. On the other was the message from Archangel Michael and the prognosis of three to six months left to live, from the specialist.

Blessed Friends

Good news came. Drunvalo Melchizedek was coming to Queensland in December 1996, to teach the Advanced Flower of Life workshop and FOL Instructor Training. Tony had been very keen to become an instructor prior to his illness. We meditated to ask our higher selves if we should go. We both got a clear yes to do the workshop. We didn't know how we would get the money, but we knew it was imperative for us to attend. The money had always arrived in the past, so we trusted that it would arrive again if the trip was in divine right order.

We had bought the house and a car based on two incomes. My income became the only source for meeting payments, and half of my time was spent caring for Tony. We were barely managing financially. Organising disability insurance payments for the mortgage meant that a mountain of forms had to be filled in and signed by various parties, and proof via doctors obtained. I felt overwhelmed and disempowered. Fortunately, practical Maggie held my hand and coached me through it all. Thank you, Maggie.

As the time drew nearer to going to Queensland, I began to worry about having enough to go. The course was nine hundred dollars each. Then there were the accommodation, airfares and food to pay for. I had earned money to pay for most of it and paid for the airfares on our newly acquired Visa cards. Out of the blue we were both offered Visa cards with no credit ratings required. Thank you Lord, thank you Jesus. Who says we are not taken care of? Wonderful timing!

All the same, with other bills to pay I was still concerned. In my meditations I was told, "Of course you are going." In one meditation Sai Baba appeared and handed me an envelope full of money.

Tony wasn't strong enough to go on our morning walks, so Diane and I would go together. This was my chance to air my fears and worries without distressing Tony. I told Diane I knew in my heart that we were meant to go and that Sai Baba had handed me some money in my meditation so I should trust that it would arrive somehow.

I was very willing to work to earn the money, but my work had dropped off. I was okay with this because I could see that Tony needed me more than we needed the money. Darling Yahoo said encouragingly, "You know it will arrive. Just trust your message from Sai Baba."

When Diane told us that she had decided to do the Flower of Life course with us, Tony and I were ecstatic.

The 7th of November was Tony's birthday. As he was still getting over his second operation, he didn't feel like a party, so we opted for a snuggly day together. Diane suggested that a few friends visit us for a cuppa in the afternoon. I explained that I had no food in the house to entertain anyone with and Tony wasn't up to it anyway. She insisted that it would just be a couple of our mates and that they would bring some goodies. Since Tony couldn't stomach birthday cake, I had just bought some nice ice cream and strawberries as a treat.

We succumbed to Diane's enthusiasm and waited in our grunging-around clothes for a couple of our friends to drop by. James and Denise arrived first, followed closely by Kate and Terrie. Within an hour we had twenty people in our home and more food and drink than would fit on the table. It was a delightful surprise, but not nearly as big as what happened later.

James, whom we love and respect immensely, put his arm around Tony and gave a heartfelt birthday speech concluding with, "... and because we all love you so much, we would like you to have this from all of us." He handed over a card and an envelope.

Tony was gob-smacked when he opened the envelope. In it was fourteen hundred dollars in cheques and cash from twenty-five of our friends. I felt an inrush of love, and my heart felt as if it would burst when I realized what they had done for us. Here was the exact remaining amount that we needed for the trip. Tony and I both burst into tears. It was such a shock. Neither of us had expected this. We felt so loved and supported, we didn't know what to say.

Apparently Maggie and Bev had secretly cooked up this idea weeks before they went overseas to see Sai Baba, leaving its implementation in Diane's capable hands. They knew I was too proud to accept money that I couldn't pay back, so they decided to give it directly to Tony as a birthday present. Diane must have been busting herself, trying not to leak any information on our walks together. There I was, rattling on about Sai Baba telling me the money was coming and to trust. I thank God every day for the love, support and selfless generosity of my friends and family.

On the way to the FOL course we stopped over in Melbourne to visit Tony's ex-wife Lyn and his two grown children, Sebastian and Giselle. This was the first time they had seen Tony since he had fallen ill. We had a lovely day together before travelling to Lloyd's place. He had magnanimously invited the three of us to stay on his beautiful property called Rainbow Springs, close to Maleny where the workshop was to be held.

Drunvalo was natural, unassuming, openhearted and genuine. The workshop was inspirational and his wife Claudette's work on the unconscious levels complemented his work beautifully. Daily, for twelve months, I had activated my Mer (counter rotating spheres of light) Ka (spirit) Ba (body) energy field as we were taught in the first FOL workshop. In the Advanced workshop, Drunvalo taught us to do partnered and group energy field activations.

When Tony and I did the partnered Mer-Ka-Ba, sitting back to back, spines aligned, tears rolled silently down my face. With this deeper connection I knew totally that Tony was dying and was choosing to go. Even though my guides had repeatedly reminded me that he was going to "go home", that I couldn't help him to heal, part of me – a big part – wanted him to live and be with me. Stuff the Divine Plan! This was one time I wished that my guidance was wrong.

The finality of the truth made me depressed and withdrawn. Tony felt my change in mood even though I tried to hide it. He knew I had received a message during the meditation and asked me what happened. For the first time ever, I told him I didn't want to tell him and I couldn't lie to him.

The course was from 9 am to 7 pm every day. Tony stuck it out for the full week. Some of it he spent lying on the floor when the pain became too much. Although it was taxing, Tony didn't want to be anywhere else. To experience sixty-four people breathing and meditating in true unity consciousness was awesome!

Major past life memories surfaced for Diane, Tony and me regarding several members of the group. They related to times in the far past when we had attempted group consciousness, planetary alignment and healing, and had failed because of egos and power struggles. We privately did several regressions and Kinesiology balances to clear these unresolved patterns. Really, the workshop was going intensively twenty-four hours a day.

It was magic to immerse ourselves in the experience of such a large, dedicated group of people working harmoniously together on their personal growth and for planetary healing.

The Mother Mountain

My guides informed me that I had to place a Galactic Wand on the top of Mt Beerwah in the Glasshouse Mountains, which are near Maleny. This was to be home for the crystal that I had tried to place in Queensland the previous year.

Before organising the climb with Patricia Athena, I asked on the inside way for permission to place the crystal on the Mother Mountain. Three Aboriginal spirits appeared. One woman was in her forties; another was in her twenties, and she carried the third spirit, a two-year-old, on her hip. The women sang to me and placed markings on my body. I had their blessing. I was told to look for an overhanging tree.

Originally Diane and I were going to go up Mt Beerwah with Patricia Athena, who had climbed it several times before. Now Zbysh and Arthur, a Jewish Canadian, were also coming. Zbysh was a vibrant 17-year old who had been Diane's partner for most of the Flower of Life workshop.

Patricia told us the Aboriginal legend which tells the story of Tibrogargan (the male mountain), his wife Beerwah and the eldest son Coonowrin (the third mountain):

One day Tibrogargan was gazing out to sea and noticed a great rising of the water. As he gathered up his younger children to take them to safety, Tibrogargan called out to Coonowrin to help his pregnant mother. Looking back, Tibrogargan was angered to see Coonowrin desert Beerwah and run off alone. The father picked up his nulla nulla (club) and struck his son, causing his crooked neck.

Feeling ashamed, Coonowrin went to his father and asked for his forgiveness, but Tibrogargan could only weep copious tears because of his son's cowardice. His tears fell to the ground and formed a stream which flowed to the sea. Tibrogargan then turned his back on Coonowrin.

Even to this day, Tibrogargan gazes far out to sea and never looks at Coonowrin. Coonowrin hangs his head in shame and his tears run off to the sea. His mother, Beerwah, is still pregnant because it takes many years to give birth to a mountain.

Patricia Athena led us in a prayer for our safety on the mountain, then we began to climb the west face of the Mother Mountain. It turned out that Diane and I wouldn't have made it up the mountain without the men. Where Diane and I were clinging desperately to the rock face on all fours, Zbysh was walking upright on two legs, no worries at all! He was like a gecko, with suction cups on his hands and feet. In places he used his hands and knees as footholds for us. He was the archetypal son, helping the mothers.

It was a stressful climb for the first third. I was challenged to stay focused and positive, and merge with the rock face. After the steep beginning, the slope evened out to a comfortable walking climb. Three quarters of the way up was Beerwah's heart, a magnificent open-mouthed cave with wonderful faces and shapes in the rocks around it. The floor of the cave was powder-soft sand. We rested there and did some toning. The young Aboriginal spirit with the child appeared and pointed in the direction to go – up and around to the east face. The crystal needed to be placed on the east face, pointing to the sea.

When we reached the top, we enjoyed spectacular views of the coast and the other mountains. Out came the mangoes from our backpacks. Arthur had never eaten a mango before – ever. Shock, horror! Poor deprived man. I love mangoes. I think they are the most delicious, sensuous fruit you can eat. I explained to Arthur that to get every ounce of pleasure out of a perfectly ripe mango, you have to snorf it first. I showed him how to reverently cradle his mango in his cupped hands and smell it for several minutes, drinking in its aroma. Art understood what I meant on the very first snorf.

"Oh! Wow!"

When the foreplay was over, Art peeled back the skin to expose the plump yellow fruit. With sweet, sticky juice running down his forearms, Art moaned with orgasmic pleasure. "Oh, God! This is a mango? Baby, where have you been all my life?"

After a feed and a drink we meditated. We activated our Mer-Ka-Ba energy fields and did unity breathing, down through the mountain to Mother Earth, around the earth and out into the cosmos. I reconnected with all the other crystals that had been placed around Australia. I saw them activated and interconnected, stabilizing the coastline with points out to sea. I saw Mt Beerwah as one huge crystal of light – truly magnificent!

After my meditation I went to look for the overhanging tree. I knew it was further down on the east face. There below me stood the woman with her child on her hip. She pointed to a straggly little tree on a thin ledge, with a sheer drop on either side of it. I was afraid if I got down there, I would not be able to get back up. I asked her on the inside way if I could place the crystal where I was. She laughed and said no. It had to be where she was.

I called up to the agile, fearless Zbysh, asking him to place the crystal for me. He called back, "No! It's your crystal. You have to place it."

Shit! He was right.

Arthur came down to where I was and said that he would hold the energy while I went down to the ledge. I inched and crab-walked down to where the Aboriginal woman was waiting. Holding on for dear life and lying on my belly, I tried to find a crevice to put the crystal in. I found a triangular gap in the rock big enough to hold the crystal. It contained just enough soil to cover it.

Climbing back was easier than anticipated. Having Arthur nearby was comforting, but in reality, if I slipped, he would not reach me in time. A fall from there would have meant a crippled body or death. I am convinced that Art was energetically helping me to stay glued to the mountain. Everyone heaved a sigh of relief when we reappeared safely back on deck.

As we headed back down the mountain, we were all very joyful and silly. We sang to Art, "Mango, mango, man. I've got to be a mango man". The Village People would have been envious of our version. Diane and Art seemed to be getting on really well. They had great fun tandem tobogganing down the flat steep parts.

The descent was easier than the ascent, except for the last

section, where I did my Mission Impossible, hanging by the fingernails, trick. At one stage I was hanging over a forty-foot drop by my fingertips with no rope and no foothold. Zbysh grabbed my hips and swung me over towards him so that I could reach a foothold and move to safety. With all of the bum-scooting I did, I finally lost the seat of my leggings to a rock.

At last we were on horizontal terra firma, and I kissed the ground with gratitude. Diane showed me the blowout she also had in her shorts. We went home to Lloyd's place to share our adventure with Tony.

Going Home

Shortly after our return to Perth, Tony took a turn for the worse. The cancer had grown again and was affecting his ability to eat. He went into Fremantle hospital for another operation. The surgeon arranged for the bile from the gall bladder to empty directly into the stomach, but he was unable to reattach the small intestine any higher up the stomach.

In order to keep the wolves from the door, I had no option but to travel overseas to teach for two weeks. This was agony for me, as Tony was in hospital, and the prognosis wasn't good. I made Tony promise that he wouldn't die while I was away, as I would never be able to forgive myself.

Once again my faithful friends Maggie and Bev went daily to the hospital to keep Tony company and to report to me his state of health. They were instructed to call me immediately if his condition worsened. I was prepared to drop everything and fly home at a moment's notice.

This was a most harrowing time, trying to stay positive and focus on my students, all the while wishing I was home taking care of my darling. The two long weeks were finally over and I returned home. As I drove into the driveway of my home I was greeted by an eagle keeping sentinel as it hovered over

145

our house.

I was relieved to be by Tony's side again. The whole time he was sick, he never complained. He was unable to eat and was fed liquid via a tube in his nose that emptied into his small intestine. Maggie smuggled in a Twinpole; an iced cordial on two pop-sticks, for Tony to suck. It was a fabulous forbidden treat, which would do him no real harm. His eyes lit up with the glee of a naughty school kid up to mischief.

Half an hour later the nurse came in to do her observations. She quietly freaked at the sight of red fluid in the bag draining Tony's stomach. Oh-oh, we hadn't thought of that!

The nurse heaved a huge sigh of relief when Tony confessed to eating a red icy pole. She admonished him for giving her such a scare! The sweetie made us promise that we would let her know if we were planning any more tricks. We figured we had better sneak in a yellow or green one next time.

The nursing staff were wonderful and gave me a lot of leeway. Often they would come in and find me curled up in bed with Tony. He found it curiously comforting and less painful if he pressed his tummy against the back of my hips. I was virtually living at the hospital, sleeping fitfully in hospital chairs – only going home to shower and change clothes. The staff eventually took pity on me and brought in a cot so that I could sleep next to Tony.

The surgeons, in their desire to maintain life at all costs, were recommending a continuation of the drip and feeding program, and even made noises about more operations. The unenviable task of calling a spade a spade was left to the hospice liaison nurse. With tears of frustration in her eyes she told Tony that he was dying. The only thing prolonging the inevitable was the drip. The options were a slow decline in hospital, or a quicker death in the comfort of our home. The finality of this news struck Tony like a shock wave, stunning him. We decided that we wanted Tony to die at home.

*

My mother had bought Tony a birdbath for Christmas. He loved to watch the magpies splashing in it and hear them carolling just outside our large bedroom window.

Terrie borrowed a portable air-conditioner from a magnanimous friend to keep Tony's room cool. She also made an exquisite butterfly and crystal ornament to support transformation, which we hung at the window. We set up a beautiful Tibetan Buddhist altar in the bedroom and I kept the offerings fresh. At Tony's request, a Buddhist monk came several times to do the appropriate prayers and ceremonies. It was a lovely peaceful sacred space.

Tony was a professional chef, so to be unable to eat or drink was doubly torturous for him. From the time that we moved in together he had chosen to be vegetarian and to abstain from alcohol like me. His sensory and gastronomic deprivation was rectified by the inventive possums, Bev and Maggie. They appeared one day and ordered me into the bedroom with Tony so I couldn't interfere with their surprise. A lot of crashing and banging in the kitchen ensued, followed by the exquisite aroma of the best quality steak money can buy, being cooked to perfection. Tony's salivary glands were cranking overtime.

A few moments later Maggie waltzed gaily in with the feast. Bev followed close behind with four of our best wine glasses and an open bottle of Hardy's pinot noir. Both had the required white linen napkin draped over one arm to dress up the occasion.

Tony was in seventh heaven, chewing the steak and savouring every ounce of flavour. When he had drained the meat of its last drop of juice he placed it on the plate and cut a fresh piece. Even though he couldn't swallow the meat it was obviously glorious just to have food in his mouth.

The wine was poured and we drank a toast. Tony was only able to have a few sips of his wine, but it did our hearts good to watch how much pleasure those few drops gave him. In fact, Maggie and Bev got such a buzz from Tony's reaction that they reappeared the next day and cooked him garlic prawns. His response was even more orgasmic than Art with the mangoes.

My friends and family taught me much in those final months of Tony's life. I had always been Miss Independent, stoically bearing problems on my own. Tony's illness was the first time in my life that I allowed myself to truly receive love and support from my friends and family, which in reality had always been waiting there for me to open up to. It finally dawned on me that I had actually been depriving my loved ones of the pleasure of the gift of giving! Watching Maggie and Bev's faces light up as they shared Tony's enjoyment of their gastronomic surprise, I realized that we were co-creating beauty and the sweetness of love amidst tragedy and loss.

*

After consulting with some nurses, Tony decided to go off all fluids to speed up the dying process. It was expected that within a week his kidneys would fail, and he would go into a coma with death following soon after.

Before he did this we contacted Tony's ex-wife Lyn and his children, Giselle and Sebastian. All three of them flew over

148

from Melbourne to stay in our house for a week. At the last moment they were given the opportunity to say what needed to be said and to complete with Tony. Tony's other daughter Amanda, who lived in England, was constantly in contact with her dad from the beginning. As she was a single mum with three teenage boys there was no spare money to fly to Australia. A friend had discussed Amanda's plight at a women's meditation group. One woman was a writer for a local newspaper and said that she would like to help. Amanda was desperate to see Tony one more time, so she contacted the newspaper lady who published a photo and large article about her situation with a request for financial support. A magnanimous stranger, Jo, lent Amanda the money for the air ticket. It took Amanda years to repay her in full.

As I wanted Amanda's arrival to be a surprise I told Tony I was going to have a massage with Terrie at her insistence. I had never taken time out for such a treat before, so I arranged for Terrie to collude with me, thereby not arousing Tony's suspicions.

I drove to the airport and picked up Amanda while Maggie held the fort. Maggie distracted Tony while we snuck Amanda into the house. I walked into the bedroom with my hands behind my back pretending to be carrying something.

"Hold out your hands and close your eyes," I said.

He complied thinking I had brought him an icy pole as a treat.

"Keep your eyes closed," I demanded.

Amanda crept into the bedroom and gently placed her hands in his. Tony opened his eyes and for a moment I regretted the surprise factor. He got such a shock I thought his heart would

149

fail him. They dissolved in tears into each other's arms.

*

From the time we returned from the Advanced Flower of Life course Tony was in a state of grace. When he slept he often had cosmic dreams of meeting intergalactic councils, and would wake up glowing. Well before he was on medication for the pain, he regularly had inspirational visions while awake. Tony became extremely sensitive to people's energy fields, and very psychic. One dear friend left our home ashen-faced after Tony told her that she would be dead in three or four years if she didn't slow down and change her lifestyle. Three years later she did indeed get breast cancer. While alone with another friend, Tony chatted with her about an affair she was having. She was flabbergasted because she hadn't told anyone!

This state of grace was infectious, causing the number of visitors to increase. Friends and family who came to pay their final respects found themselves drawn back again and again. To experience someone dying with genuinely no fear was inspirational. Tony's connection to God was so palpable that *Going Home* as he called it really was a natural, loving event.

We cherished every moment we had together. Our song was *"Have I Told You Lately (That I Love You)?"* by Van Morrison. We would play it over and over as we danced, holding each other tenderly and crying. I tried to be brave but at times like these I would break down.

We both knew that we would maintain a spiritual connection after his death because we believed that consciousness continues after the death of the body. That wasn't an issue. I was going to miss his physical presence. One time when we were sitting holding hands, he turned to me and said, "I don't want you to be alone when I am gone. I will send you someone special, a good man to be with."

Wanting to be complete on all levels, Tony asked James to oversee the funeral arrangements. Tony wrote a poem for the funeral service, which James recorded on tape so that we would be able to hear his voice one last time. Tony chose the words he wanted spoken and the music for his cremation. It was Van Morrison's *"Bright Side of the Road."* Kate, a lovely and talented artist, painted a special healing picture to support his being complete with his life. Many people from Tony's past, whom he had long ago lost contact with, called out of the blue to say goodbye. It was a very stressful yet beautiful time.

Just before Tony went into a coma we all shared a magic day together. On this day he seemed to be granted the gift of strength and divine grace to do the things he loved one last time. First up, with Bev and Maggie being chef's assistants, Tony cooked us all brunch. He dished up eggs, mushrooms, tomatoes, beans and toast, with bacon for the carnivores. Lynn, Giselle, Sebastian, Amanda, Maggie, Bev, Diane, Tony and myself – what a mob to feed!

We all then headed bush to the state forest behind Diane's house. Although we had brought the wheel chair, Tony insisted on walking all the way along the track as we took turns supporting his arm. The weather was made to order, with the canopy of trees softening the brightness of the midmorning sun. Lots of laughter and reminiscing was stimulated by the bitter-sweetness of sharing this last walk with his nearest and dearest.

After an afternoon sleep, Bev, Maggie, Tony and I went to the movies to see *Michael*, starring John Travolta. Since Archangel

Michael had been with us all through this journey, it seemed fitting to see a movie about him. Needless to say we loved the movie, but the ending had Tony and me looking at each other in amazement. As Michael was going back to heaven, the song playing was *"Bright Side of the Road"* by Van Morrison! This was the song Tony had chosen to be played as his coffin went to be cremated.

It was wonderful how Tony's energy held up for this remarkable gift of a day.

*

After a week with Tony, Lyn, Sebastian and Amanda flew to their respective homes. It had been very special for Tony to have his whole family with him. Giselle decided that she would stay until the end. A few days later Tony went into a coma with his eyes wide open. Regularly I would irrigate his dry expressionless eyes and swab his parched mouth. I massaged and turned him periodically in an attempt to keep him as comfortable as possible.

On one of his visits the monk spent some time counselling Giselle. Afterwards he asked me if I would mind a healing space being set up for Giselle, Sebastian, Amanda and Lynn as they had not yet fully dealt with the imminence of Tony's transition. I agreed that it was a good idea.

To prepare the healing space the monk asked me for photographs of the family. I left Giselle to go through the albums and pick out photos meaningful for her while I tended to some housework. When I came back into our bedroom I found the monk finishing a ceremony and Giselle putting up photos above our bed.

The whole energy of the room had changed from that of restful peace and nurturing to intense stress and chaos. All of the family's unresolved issues now bombarded and crowded out the room. Energetically there was no longer any space for Tony and me.

"Why did you set it up in here?" I asked incredulously.

"This is the best place," he replied.

"I think it would be far better in the lounge room," I protested.

"Well it's done now," he said, and headed out of the house, preventing any further discussion.

I sat on our bed next to Tony and surveyed the situation. There were photos of Tony's ex-wife Lynn, all his children and numerous other people as well, all across the head of our bed.

"Giselle, I won't be able to sleep with all this going on in here. Let's move it to the lounge room."

"No way; the monk thinks this is the best place so it is staying here!" she retorted. Clearly I had no authority in my own home as far as Giselle was concerned.

"At least let's put the photos across the room on the cupboard," I said meeting her half way.

"No, they are just where I want them. They stay where they are!" In her mind the matter was settled and she left the room. I followed her out to the back of the house.

"Giselle, the energy in the room has completely changed. It is horrible and stressful now. How can that be helpful to Tony? He's spent the last eight months doing his letting go and clearing the decisions and traumas in his life which led him to this point. It's unfair that you expect him to have to deal with all the family's unresolved stuff. It's not his responsibility to do it for you. Let's move the pictures over to the other side of the room so that Tony is free to let go when he is ready and I'll be able to sleep."

"It's you who has the problem, Patti. I'm happy with the way things are," Giselle said dismissively.

It was the weirdest feeling when I returned to my bedroom; there was so much psychic noise in the room I couldn't think straight. I sat on the bed in great distress.

To my astonishment Tony pulled himself out of the coma, sat upright and said, "What's wrong, honey?"

As I was searching for words to explain the situation, Tony turned and looked at all the photographs and asked, "What is my ex-girlfriend doing there? Where are the pictures of you, me and Adam and Craig? You are my family now."

God, what a relief! He had hauled himself back to consciousness just to resolve the problem. Tony must have, on some level, heard our conversation because he then said, "Please move the photos over to the cupboard door."

I complied happily with his request; then Tony fell back, exhausted, into a coma again. This was the last time we spoke.

One week later Tony was still alive. Early one evening, the Buddhist monk arrived and was convinced that Tony was about to pass over due to his laboured breathing. He had been present at many transitions and knew the signs. I was beside myself with distress because I was convinced that he wasn't ready to go, but was waiting for something, and that he was in a lot of pain. The monk ignored me, continuing with the ceremony and appropriate prayers.

A battle of wills ensued between us. I wanted Tony to be turned and made comfortable, as I was feeling his pain and distress. The monk wanted Tony left as he was. It felt similar to a doctor inducing the birth of a baby for no other reason than his own convenience. He had decided that Tony was making his transition now and that was that. It was almost as if he was willing him to go. Maggie and Bev were so upset by him that they left the bedroom rather than interfere. Giselle believed that the monk knew better than I, and that I was the one holding on, not releasing Tony. I sobbed with exhaustion and anguish at having my authority and inner knowing challenged so powerfully after weeks of lack of sleep. The last thing I wanted was a full-blown argument at such an important moment for Tony.

Fortunately Bev bustled everyone out of the room when things came to a head. Maggie came in, sat next to Tony and held his hand. As I looked on, Maggie said, "Tony, if you can hear me, blink your eyes."

Amazingly Tony slowly closed then opened his eyes! He had not done that the whole time he was in a coma.

"If you are in pain, blink your eyes." He blinked again.

"Do you want some morphine?" He blinked slowly again.

"Right, that settles it," said Maggie as she strode off to ring the nurse.

The monk went home. The hospice nurse gave Tony some morphine, then helped me to turn him and make him comfortable. Soon the household was quiet and I calmed down, knowing Tony was no longer in pain. Later I said to

Maggie, "Tony seems to be waiting for something. I'm sure of it." That something arrived a few days later in the mail. It was a letter of love and reconciliation from Tony's estranged mother, Phyllis.

I sat next to Tony, leaned close and read his mother's letter out loud to him. When I finished reading I looked at Tony. Although his expression was deadpan with vacant eyes, tears were rolling gently down both his cheeks. He had heard every word, and he was complete.

That night the house was soothingly calm. We were strangely at peace as if we all silently knew tonight was the night and all was in divine right order. For the first time in ages we all felt like eating a proper meal. Bev, Maggie, Giselle and I went to bed early. I lay down next to Tony and slept soundly. Around midnight I suddenly woke up and I knew that Tony had just made his transition (26th February 1997).

Crystal Children

The "spiritual" way is to release your loved ones on all levels, including mentally and emotionally, so that their spirits are free. I genuinely thought I had done that, but I was really just numb. My feelings were disowned and stuffed down, so that Tony would be able to move on and I could get on with the practicalities of my life.

Five months after Tony's death I felt a presence in my bed. Tony cuddled into my back just as he used to do when he was alive. I told him to go and that he shouldn't be here. He told me that he would not leave me until I did my grieving. Tony refused to go until I allowed myself to feel again.

His presence was strong, and I missed him so much, that on the third night of his visits, the dam of my welled-up emotions broke. I couldn't believe the sounds that were coming out of me. They were coming up from my very toenails in the form of loud, gut-wrenching wails and moans, like those of Eastern European women at funerals.

I knew that any strong emotion denied for long enough would eventually wreak havoc mentally or physically, so I surrendered to the process. I cried for two weeks until there was nothing left to cry. I became a recluse; I didn't want or need anyone around me. Tony was with me periodically through this process, stimulating deeper levels of emotion and letting go.

During this time, Corrie, a close friend of Tony, rang me to see how I was faring. She and her five-year-old daughter Jessie used to share a house with Tony when we were first going out together.

"Patti, I've been feeling Tony around a lot for about a week and I was ignoring it," Corrie confided. "Then this morning Jessie came into my bedroom and complained that she was tired because Tony woke her up and talked all night to her."

I sat silently, stunned, and listened as Corrie continued. "When I asked what Tony had talked to her about, Jessie said that he wanted to let me know that he was okay and he was happy. Then he started to cry and said he had to go because Patti was sad."

I didn't know what to say.

"I feel that because he couldn't get me to listen to him, Tony resorted to talking to Jessie. I think Tony was trying to let me know that you were deeply depressed and he wanted me to check on you."

"Yeah, I have been rather low and missing him a lot lately," I confessed.

Even in death Tony was looking after me.

Raylene's children were also woken up several times by Tony's visiting them during the night to tell them that he was well and happy. Ashley is very psychic and often was afraid at night because of people (spirits) visiting her and disturbing her sleep. Ashley said that she went to a spaceship with Tony and he gave her a symbol to protect her at night. When Raylene asked her to draw the symbol, she drew a Star of David. The three dimensional version of this is the Mer-Ka-Ba, which we use in the Flower of Life meditations.

Sai Baba was another friend that Ashley said visited her often. She really liked him and to her he was John. Whenever she saw a photo of Baba she said, "That's my friend John."

*

Children have traditionally been able to see things their parents can't, or have "imaginary" friends. Unfortunately ,the disbelief of the parents usually causes these gifts to be forgotten as the children grow up. Raylene was not one of these parents. She always gave her children the benefit of the doubt. Just because she couldn't see or hear what they were experiencing, didn't mean that it wasn't real. Raylene shared with me several stories about her kids:

When Ashley was two–and-a-half she looked at her mother with a curious expression on her face. Raylene asked her what was wrong. Ashley looked at Raylene's belly and said, "Mummy you have a baby girl in your tummy."

"No, mummy isn't pregnant darling," she stammered. Raylene had been taking precautions, as she very definitely wasn't ready for another baby just yet!

"Yes you are," Ashley countered emphatically.

A week later Raylene missed her period. Several weeks later it was confirmed that she was pregnant. In due course Raylene gave birth to her second daughter, Shatika.

*

Around the same time, little Ashley was walking with her mother through the bush near their home in the Armadale hills.

Ashley said, "See the funny monkeys hiding behind the trees?"

Raylene couldn't see anything but trusted that Ashley was seeing something so she just replied, "That's interesting, sweetie."

A few days later Ashley called Raylene over to the TV and said "See, mummy. There are the monkeys I saw!" The program was about Aborigines. Ashley was seeing the Aboriginal spirits in the bush. All of the area where they lived once was tribal land.

*

While Raylene was pregnant with Shatika, Ashley nearly drowned, then had one serious accident or illness after another. It was as if she was trying to leave the planet. Raylene said she had had a secret fear of losing Ashley from the time she was born. While breast-feeding her, Raylene would often cry with irrational thoughts of losing her.

When her condition became critical a friend, Louise, offered to do some healing for Ashley. She said that Ashley was the survivor of a set of triplets and she had made a pact to die and be with the other two spirits.

Louise prayed to God and asked for the two baby spirits to be escorted to the light and back to heaven so that Ashley could be free to live her life. The contract was broken. Ashley actually sat up and waved goodbye to her siblings.

A few days latter Ashley hugged her mother's pregnant tummy

and said, "Please baby, please come now. You will make me better!"

That night Raylene went into labour and Shatika was born two months premature. To this day the sisters are very close.

*

Ashley's friend was a little blue fairy called Jimeny. One day Raylene observed her daughter dodging left and right as she sat on the lounge watching TV. Finally, in frustration, Ashley yelled, "Jimeny, get out of the way!" Apparently the little blue fairy was flying around in front of her, obscuring the view of her favourite program.

Raylene's son Raymond also had a friend, called Squidgy. He was rather ugly, with a big nose and ears. Raylene showed me a photograph of Ashley and Raymond playing together. Clearly discernable in the photo with them are their friends Squidgy and Jimeny!

*

Raylene's cousin was due to have twins. Out of the blue Ashley said, "Jimeny has gone to be with Amanda because she is having the babies now." About ten minutes later there was a phone call and Raylene was told that Amanda had gone into labour.

A little while later Raylene asked Ashley if Jimeny was still with Amanda. "No," she replied "Jimeny has taken the babies to heaven."

Horrified, Raylene rang the hospital and discovered that the twins had indeed both died.

A while later Raylene asked Ashley, "Where is Jimeny now?"

"Oh, Jimeny is with the mummy because she is very sad."

*

These psychic children are becoming the norm rather than the exception as humanity evolves, allowing us to see, hear and experience on more subtle levels.

Have you noticed that your intuition is more accurate lately? Can you "read" people more easily, knowing what they are thinking, and when they are not being totally honest with you? Does the plight of others suffering on the other side of the world affect you more deeply these days? Is your conscience bugging you more often? The adults are waking up too!

Thousands of people from my generation have sown the seeds for a peaceful reality and environmental balance, faithfully following their spiritual guidance and being proactive in different ways, doing personal development work and connecting up with others through worldwide prayers and meditations.

Many people over the last thirty years have felt compelled to take rocks and crystals to sacred sites, heal the energy lines of the Earth, using the focus of their minds and hearts to create and maintain an electromagnetic grid of love and higher consciousness around the planet.

The seeds have grown and borne fruit in our grandchildren. On James Twyman's web site, he writes about the children around the world who communicate telepathically with each other and who have created a grid of love around the Earth. These children apparently are born knowing that they are emissaries of Love and Light for humanity. I believe our children and grandchildren, now more than ever before, are our teachers; and many are more conscious and evolved than us.

Lee Carroll, Jan Tober and Doreen Virtue have written about the Indigo children, so named for the indigo blue in their auras (the subtle energy field around the body). This is the colour for the third eye chakra, which regulates clairvoyance, the ability to see spirits and read peoples' energy fields.

The next generation, mostly born after 2000, are the Crystal children who apparently have opalescent auras, with pastel hues. They are peaceful and loving, and have a fascination for crystals and rocks. These Crystal children have a unity consciousness; know their soul purpose, and their part in co-creating heaven on earth.

Humanity is beginning to experience interdimensionally, beyond three-dimensional physical reality. This is not achieved by thinking outside the box; it is achieved by removing the box altogether. The box is our fears, rigid beliefs, sense of isolation, and self-imposed limitations. I experience pain in my life when I hold on to limiting patterns of behaviour and beliefs, way beyond their use-by date. It takes a lot of diligence to continuously bring myself back from the illusion of separation, to the reality that we are all one interconnected, holographic consciousness. I do this by endeavouring to live my life by the golden rule: *Do unto others as you would have them do unto you*. Being a human crystal, anchoring Love and Light on the planet, does not exempt one from the travails of ordinary life, but it gives extra strength to endure.

Life Goes On

After Tony died I attempted to resurrect my business in Perth. My client base had dwindled, and class numbers were down. It became increasingly difficult to pay my mortgage. I discussed with several friends the fact that I might have to look for a different job. Maybe I could go back to working in land care and whole farm planning, or teaching dance and aerobics as I had a Diploma in Dance Studies.

"I could become a secretary!" I joked to Maggie. She would snort back a laugh at the thought of me dying of boredom in an office.

"Don't worry, something will come up, Patti," she'd say reassuringly.

By September, things were getting financially desperate. With tears of frustration I sat in my office and scanned my bills. I looked up to the heavens and yelled to the universe, "I am willing to work but the work isn't there! I do everything you ask of me, so how about helping me now! I need a steady income to take the pressure off me. I am willing to do anything."

Ten minutes later the telephone rang. "Hi, Patti, it's Flora here." Flora ran the WA School of Reflexology with Lynn, an old professional dancing buddy of mine. "I was at Barry Harwood's Study Centre today. An advert on his board caught my eye and I immediately thought of you. You have a Diploma in Massage, don't you?"

"Yes."

"You taught massage?" Flora enquired.

"Yes I taught at TAFE (Technical College) and at APACE with a government-funded project. Why?"

"Mandara Spa in Bali is looking for a Spa trainer to teach their staff. They'll train you in their techniques for one month in Bali, then send you to where you are needed in Asia. With your qualifications in Kinesiology and massage you'd be perfect for the job, surely."

I took down the details of the advert, revamped my Curriculum Vitae, and applied for the job. I had asked the boys upstairs for some help and in ten minutes an answer was given. I was stunned by how quickly everything fell into place. I got the job and was in Bali, training, within three weeks.

This job was perfect for me: good pay with set hours in a relaxing tropical environment. I shared a house in the middle of rice fields with Noor, another Australian trainer who had lived in Indonesia for years. She was easy to get on with and was very helpful showing me the ropes.

After one month learning Balinese Massage, two-people massage and body scrubs unique to Mandara Spa, I was transferred to The Datai Hotel, in Langkawi. This place was heaven. Beautiful luxury rooms overlooked the forest and the two swimming pools overlooked the sea. For three months I worked in Malaysia for

165

Mandara Spa. Being in such a soothing natural setting helped me to regain my strength and belief that all was well in my world. It really was a perfect gift from the gods.

When the training there was complete my contract ran out. At the same time the Indonesian economy went through the floor. Instead of expanding to other places as planned, Mandara Spa decided to suspend all new projects for a while. I returned to Perth.

*

There are so many ways that you can learn to see and hear guidance from the angels and other Light beings. One thing that I have learnt is that first you have to ask for help. The angels have a policy of non-interference unless a person asks out loud for guidance. Be warned! They know when you mean it and when your intentions are all hot air.

Angels manifest to you in accordance with your disposition and belief system. My angels know that the best way to get my attention is through irreverent humour or practical straight talking. The flowery stuff turns me off.

If I have been gnashing my gums over wanting to make some changes in my life, they appear to me smoking cigarettes and sipping a mug of coffee with their feet up on the table! The angels casually look in my direction and ask, "Oh, you mean it now, do you?"

Humour works well with me, especially when I am taking myself too seriously. I only honour guidance that is encouraging, positive and not harmful to myself or others. Anything else I consider to be my mind and ego playing games, and I disregard it.

Whenever the angels want me to agree to do something, I am requested to state out loud three times whatever it is I agree to. "I, Patricia Leahy-Shrewsbury, do agree to ....." Three times seems to be significant when doing things in relationship to the angels. Also they ask permission every time before they do any energetic work with/on me.

Archangel Michael, for many people, is full of peace, love and light. I call him part of the kick-arse crew. For me Michael has always been the messenger of hard truths and practical advice, such as, "Tony has chosen to die"; or, "Today I want you to do a Kinesiology balance to improve your relationship with your sister"; or, "Please go on a ten-day juice fast with an enema every day".

When I turned thirty I made a commitment to myself that my personal development and spiritual growth was my primary goal in life. Everything had to be in alignment with that aim: my work, relationships, and lifestyle. When you make that sort of choice the spiritual ground rules change. When you think you are going left the divine plan sends you right. An example of this occurred in early 1998.

Diane asked me if I would like to do a trip to Nepal, trek over the Himalayas into Tibet and do the *kora* (circumambulation) around Mount Kailash, then trek back over the mountains to Nepal. The whole trek would take a month and four-thousand dollars.

Mount Kailash (also spelt Kailas) is the most sacred mountain to Buddhists, Hindus, Jains and Bon Pos. A pilgrimage to and walking around Mt Kailash is said to erase one lifetime of karma. Bathing in Lake Manasarovar, which is near the mountain, clears the karma for seven generations.

Diane's intention was to attract a group of like-minded people to do planetary healing throughout the trek. Mt. Kailash is considered to be the navel of the Earth according to the guide books, although many westerners say it is the crown chakra of the planet. Either way there was agreement that it was sacred and a major power place.

This sort of trip sounded inviting, but the practicalities were that I couldn't afford to take a month off work, being self-employed. I declined Diane's offer and headed overseas to teach Kinesiology.

Thanks to the generosity and great organising skills of my sponsors, my classes went well, and I had ample money to buy a laptop computer. With all the travelling I was doing it seemed essential that I get one. While overseas I stopped over in Kuala Lumpur and visited Karen, a valued friend of many years. Karen's husband Balwinder worked for a computer firm so I asked his advice. As I was computer illiterate, I left the choice of laptop and the money to buy it in his capable hands.

I mentioned to Karen that during this trip to Malaysia I really wanted to meet Sister Jennie Seah who was the lady involved with the Quan Yin pearls. Quan Yin is the Chinese Goddess of mercy and has similar qualities to Mother Mary in the Catholic religion. Many people in Perth were wearing Quan Yin pearls for protection. The pearls are caged in thin threads of gold and worn on a necklace; some people's pearls continue growing larger after they receive them. Apparently the pearls manifested on statues of Quan Yin on Jennie's altar in her home. This I wanted to see first hand.

Patrick, a fellow Kinesiologist who regularly visited and worked with Sister Jennie and the monks, had given me Jennie's contact number. I gave the phone number to Karen to see if she could get hold of Jennie. Karen rang me that evening and said excitedly, "I've spoken to Sister Jennie, and she would like to meet us! The catch is that she flies to New Zealand in two days to teach Reiki. We have to fly up there tomorrow for the day if we want to see her. Jennie won't be back from New Zealand until after you go back to Perth, so our only chance is tomorrow."

"Let's both meditate and ask if it is appropriate to go," I suggested.

"Okay," said Karen and hung up the phone. Ten minutes later Karen rang back.

"Well, what did you get?" she asked expectantly.

"Quan Yin came into my meditation and asked me to go. What was your answer?"

"Oh, me too. Isn't that great?"

"How on earth are we going to get plane tickets at nine at night, for early tomorrow?"

"I'll look into it," said Karen.

By 11 pm Karen, with the help of her wonderful husband, had arranged and paid for two air tickets to Penang, and confirmed with Jennie that we would be arriving at 6 am. Jennie magnanimously offered to drive over from the mainland and pick us up at Penang airport.

True to her word, she was waiting for us. She gave us a leisurely tour of all the main Buddhist temples in Penang. The temples were beautifully maintained, with ornate decorations and huge serene gold statues of Buddha dominating the rooms. Karen and I meditated under a huge Banyan tree growing in the grounds of one of the temples.

While we were driving from one place to the next, Jennie shared her story with us. As she had been a very sickly child, her parents took her to see Sai Baba in India, and he was able to heal her. In the following years as she was growing up she had several visits to Sai Baba, who took Jennie under his wing.

"See this ring; Sai Baba manifested this ring for me." The ring was gold with a large stone in it. "He manifested this one too," Jennie said matter-of-factly as she pointed to another ring with different precious stones in it.

Jennie then held up the necklace she was wearing. It was a crucifix made of diamonds.

"This was given to me by Mother Theresa. It was a present to her from someone. Mother Theresa doesn't believe in having material possessions, so she gave it to me. She gives all gifts like this away to people."

"Lady Di was there too with Mother Theresa, a few months before she died. I was with them both."

Karen and I eyed each other and shifted uncomfortably in our seats. I quietly decided to give Jennie the benefit of the doubt and stay open-minded. Maybe she really was an exceptional woman who had met some extraordinary people in her life.

Jennie invited us to a sumptuous vegetarian meal at a local Buddhist restaurant. After lunch we drove over the bridge to Jennie's home in Butterworth, West Malaysia. It consisted of a tiny lounge opening into the indoor/outdoor wet kitchen and dining area. A door went off the lounge to the rest of the house. The cooking area had a corrugated tin roof which was drawn back so the area was open to the sky.

In one corner of this busy room was an altar. To say it dominated the room is an understatement. There were food offerings, candles, about a dozen Quan Yin statues covered with pearls and pink *vibhuti*, statues of Buddha with gold *vibhuti* and several large pictures of Sathya Sai Baba.

One large photograph of Sai Baba was completely covered with *vibhuti*; only Baba's face was showing. I looked closely at it, wondering how the grey sacred ash could stay so thickly on the photograph. There was so much *vibhuti* manifesting on Baba's picture that a metal tray was secured to the wall to catch it all. The wall between the photograph and the tray was also covered in grey ash.

A photo of a statue of Krishna had its own tray to catch the red *vibhuti* manifesting on it. Below these two miracles was another large photo of Sai Baba. The bottom half of it was saturated, staining the picture orange. A bowl below the picture caught the liquid seeping from it.

"That's *amrita*, nectar of the Gods, materializing on Baba's photograph," Jennie explained.

I had read and heard many stories of pious devotees being rewarded for their faith with the materialization of sacred ash, Sai Baba's calling card, on pictures on their shrines. What I witnessed at Jennie's seemed like overkill.

"All this started when a friend who was dying of cancer visited me and prayed for hours in front of this altar. After several days of praying to be healed, the man coughed up something small and hard. When he examined it he discovered to his consternation that it was a pearl. He gave it to me, and, I put the pearl on a Quan Yin statue. After this incident the man was free from cancer," said Jennie. "Overnight a second pearl grew. I was amazed! This phenomenon has continued from that day on."

"I had heard that monks pray over the pearls, giving them extra potency. Is that true?" I enquired.

"Yes; there is a group of monks that I help with donations of food and money. I take the manifested pearls to the monks, and they pray over them as they continue growing. Some people pay for these healing, protecting pearls. They give us their name, address, and birth date, and the monks pray for them. Each pearl is placed in a glass of water and sinks to the bottom of the glass. One person's details are put with each pearl. When it is time for the pearls to go to their new owners, the pearl floats to the top of the water and stays there."

Karen developed a headache and went quite pale. I suggested that Karen sit down, relax and meditate in front of the shrine while I gave Jennie a Kinesiology balance to assist her with a problem she was having.

Jennie and I rejoined Karen after the session. Jennie leaned over and peered at a photo of Sai Baba.

"Did you see this, Karen?" Jennie asked pointing to Baba. We both looked closer.

"Oh my God!" gasped Karen. "Will you look at that?"

Running down from Sai Baba's mouth, on the outside of the glass, was a thick stream of *amrita*! It continued to run as we watched. Alarm bells went off in my head as the sceptic in me woke up with a vengeance. I searched for tiny holes but the glass was intact. I thought that maybe Jennie had squirted some substance onto the glass when she bent over. I quickly dismissed that theory as I had watched her the whole time; besides, she had a short-sleeved shirt on and nothing in her hands.

"I was praying all the time you were busy with Jennie for a sign or proof that all this manifesting is real," commented Karen in consternation.

I decided I wanted to pay for a Quan Yin pearl ($60 AUS). Jennie warned that paying the money didn't guarantee that I would receive a pearl in the mail. "If your pearl doesn't rise to the surface of the water it won't be sent to you."

She took my details for the monks to pray over. I figured if I was meant to receive one it would arrive in divine time. The day I had had with Jennie was enough; a pearl would just be a bonus. Karen also gave Jennie some money and her family's details.

We gathered our gear and hopped in the car, as it was time to catch our flight back to Kuala Lumpur. We were quiet and reflective on the drive back to the airport. What a day we had experienced. I certainly had gotten far more than I had bargained for. Karen and I thanked Jennie for the wonderful day and said our goodbyes.

On the plane we discussed what had happened. "I still have a headache from it all," groaned Karen. "Part of me feels like I have been severely conned. I just can't get my head around it all."

"My mind feels like it's been stretched a little too much, too," I admitted. "Well, let's look at it this way. Jennie went out of her way to spend the day with us, the day before she has to fly overseas. She drove to the airport to pick us up and drop us off again; it would have cost us a lot to do that all by taxi. She gives us a wonderful free lunch and a full guided tour of Penang, then she invites us into her home. If nothing else, she has been incredibly generous on all levels. At no time has Jenny asked us for money." I went over the day's events in my mind. "As for the manifesting of the *amrita*, my mind is having difficulty digesting it even though I saw it with my own eyes."

Back in Kuala Lumpur I thanked Karen for arranging our little adventure and thanked Balwinder for his offer of finding me a computer.

"It'll be waiting for you when you get back from Singapore in three days' time, Patti," he promised.

I caught the train to Singapore to attend a Kinesiology workshop with Carla Hannaford. As usual, Carla's course was informative and inspiring. It was wonderful to catch up with Moira, a fellow Aussie who had worked in Asia for many years, doing primary school teaching and Kinesiology. Sumi and Hadi; Muslim friends who ran a Brain Gym-based school accompanied Moira and me to have a yummy meal in Little India and explore the night markets.

On the return train trip to Kuala Lumpur I was enjoying the exuberance of a group of French university students sharing my compartment when my guides butted in.

"We are cancelling your computer; we want you to go to Tibet."

When I arrived in Kuala Lumpur Balwinder gave me back my money and apologized profusely for his inability to get me a computer. Apparently the laptop I wanted was not in stock, and there was not another comparable model available for that price.

So I went to Tibet.

Tibet

Diane was ecstatic that I was coming with her on the trek. We sat in her office going over the details of the trip.

"Look at this," said Diane animatedly. "This lady Chandara runs Earth Link Mission, a group that does planetary alignments. They are opening a Stargate in Tibet at the time we are going to be on Mount Kailash!"

She handed me an Earth Link Mission newsletter containing channelled information from The Twelfth High Council Ancient of Days.

> The three teams of beings who have dedicated themselves to this mission are in place and ready to align the energies. They are located in Mongolia, Tibet and China, forming a triangulation of light which will open and access the HEART energies of the Christ Consciousness.
>
> The main intention and purpose of this Stargate alignment is to bring harmony, peace, love, light and understanding in reuniting the energies of the world's religious belief systems into the Unity consciousness with which they were created.
>
> ....This awakening will return the personal responsibility to each and every human on the planet. They will begin once

again to know and remember personal choice, personal commitment and personal responsibility for the creation of their lives.

In another article, The Twelfth High Council Ancient of Days gave more information about the Tibet Stargate:

We would speak with you now of the work which will involve the Atlantean energies in combination with the Tibet Stargate Alignment. At this time the final resonance repatterning of the Atlantean Crystalline grid systems will be accomplished.

...This is a time of coordinated efforts globally.

...The activation of these crystalline grid systems is the key that they have been awaiting. The consciousness is for the good of all and harm of none.

The information contained in Chandara's newsletter excited me greatly. Here was an organised group of people doing crystalline grid alignment and activation similar to what I was doing. It reminded me that when "an idea's time has come", it will inspire diverse people from all over the world to bring it forward into physical manifestation. If some people ignore the call, there are others who will heed it. Similarly, major inventions are never discovered by just one person. The trend is that several scientists from different countries simultaneously create new inventions, discoveries and theories. It is just a matter of who gets to the patent office first to have their name attached to the invention.

I suggested to Diane that we email Chandara and inform her that we were going to Tibet at that time. Chandara promptly emailed Diane back saying that she was not able to physically go to Tibet this time and was doing the activation from the United States.

We volunteered to link up energetically with her group at a set time and day. Chandara had a crystal wand that she used at the energy centre activations around the world and it had recently been used in Stargate activation in Australia. She generously offered for us to take it and some vials of essences to assist us in Tibet.

As he lived closer, Chandara sent the essences and wand to Art. Art was partnering Diane on this trip and had organised for three Americans, Michael, Tracy and Dr Raju, to come with us. The final count of people was nine for the trek – five from Australia, one Canadian (Art) and three from the USA.

Wow! Arrangements were falling into place smoothly. My sister Wendy lent me her snow jacket, and I bought thermal underwear, a backpack and sturdy hiking boots. I waterproofed my boots several times, then set out to break them in and get fit. Diane and I went for long brisk walks along the beach. I just about wore out my butt and the step machine at the gym, but I still was not sure that I would have the stamina for trekking over mountains for a month. There are no mountains and definitely no snow in Western Australia, so I had no idea how I would handle the cold and the climb. My mind was buzzing with excited anticipation. Roughing it in a tent would be no problem; I was used to camping and I love being in the wilderness.

Diane organised a meal at a Chinese restaurant so that the Australian contingent for the trek could meet. Melvin, Diane's brother, was there. What a sweet, gentle-natured man he is. Next to him was Lana, a tall, bespectacled part-Maori woman with a ready smile, a low heh, heh, heh sort of laugh and long dark wild hair like Diane's. A little while later, the attractive, introspective Yolande arrived. She had just completed an eight-week-long walk along the Bibbulmun Track through the beautiful forests of southwest WA, with fellow supporters of the environment.

We took turns to introduce ourselves and share why we chose to do this trip.

"I just woke up one morning and announced to my partner, 'I'm going to Tibet and Nepal.' My partner looked at me with consternation and said, 'My God, you're serious, aren't you?' A few days later Diane's advert in Nova magazine jumped out at me, so I rang her up. I had no money, but I was sure this trip was something I had to do," said Lana. "I tried all sorts of schemes to raise the funds, but no luck. I was really starting to sweat on it as the deadline for payment was getting close. Then on the last day for signing up I had three different offers to pay for my trip. Not one but three!" Lana grinned.

"It's meant to be, meant to be," confirmed Diane nodding.

We all bombarded Diane with questions about logistics and what to expect regarding food and conditions. For many of us this was promising to be an adventure of a lifetime.

Surprisingly, my guides gave me no weird instructions to prepare me for Tibet as they had for my Kimberley trip. My backpack was packed to bursting point. I was travelling with limited funds, but as the boys upstairs had asked me to go to Tibet, I knew that all was in divine right order and I would be taken care of.

*

We arrived at Kathmandu airport, Nepal, where drivers greeted us and took us to the Nirvana Gardens Hotel. I hastily unpacked and went to Art and Diane's room. Art had arrived the day before. It was so good to have the three of us together again. I hadn't seen Art since he was in our home, just before Tony died. We all talked at once, having conversations on six different topics simultaneously.

Art reverently unwrapped and showed us Chandara's power stick, which was about three feet long, painted dark green, with a single terminator three-inch quartz crystal mounted on the top. What looked like kangaroo hide secured the crystal and formed a hand grip one third of the way from the top of the shaft. Nine different stones such as citrine and black tourmaline were attached to the wand. Carved into the shaft were a Star of David and the Egyptian Eye of Horus. With it were vials of Star Essences which were to be placed in the headwaters of three major rivers in Tibet.

We shared the guidance that each of us had obtained from meditations regarding the purpose of the trip. It was obvious that although we were there to do group planetary healing, we were each going to experience profound personal challenges and transformation. Of the nine participants, five were on the trek to do the planetary healing: Art, Diane, Michael, Tracy and I. We met in Art and Diane's room to meditate together and share our insights.

Michael turned out to be a fashion-conscious, very fit, dancer, actor and manager of a trendy restaurant in San Francisco. He had been receiving information from the spirit of Padmasambhava, the father of Tibetan Buddhism, with whom Art also had an affinity. Padmasambhava was a learned Tantric saint of Northern India who was invited to Tibet by King Thi-Sron Detsan in the middle of the eighth century. He spent fifty years teaching the Tantra doctrine of Buddhism and founding monasteries in Tibet. I had a connection with Maitreya Buddha, the future Buddha who is expected to come to earth four thousand years after the disappearance of Gautama Siddhartha Buddha, for the deliverance of all sentient beings. Maitreya means loving kindness, and his colour is yellow. He kept appearing in my meditations but there was no dialogue.

I had virtually no knowledge of the many gods and goddesses of Tibetan Buddhism at that time. I decided to not buy any books about them, or where we would be travelling, so that they would not distort or influence my meditations.

Tracy is an earthy, straight-talking promotions director. She was guided to bring with her information about the four directions of the indigenous North Americans. In true synchronicity, for months prior to this trip Tracy was also receiving guidance from Padmasambhava in her meditations.

We recorded the various details from each person and agreed to honour everyone's input and remain open as to how it all tied together. This way we would create the space for magic to happen.

*

Exploring Kathmandu over the next few days, as we acclimatized to the altitude, was loads of fun. I enjoyed window-shopping for brightly dyed shawls, stunning jewellery, locally crafted hats and thick wool jumpers. It was a shame that my finances and lack of luggage space prevented me from buying much. My only purchases were a sandalwood Buddhist rosary and a light-purple, traditional woollen hat with flaps over the ears, which I was sure would be a lifesaver in the cold of the mountains.

I wished many times that my sons were with me, as they would have been right at home in the relaxed, exotic atmosphere. The street vendors were always polite, dignified, open and smiling. No one ever hassled me to buy their wares as they had in India.

In spite of Diane's warning to drink only bottled water and to avoid raw salads and vegetables, we found KC's Restaurant where it was safe to eat whatever we wanted. The food in Kathmandu was great, so I enjoyed it while I could! I knew that being vegetarian in the wilderness was going to be a challenge for me and our cooks on the trek.

Most of what we wanted to see was within walking distance, such as the busy local market place in Durbar Square, and Swayambhu Stupa perched high on a hill above the city. The two-thousand-year-old Stupa is said to be the chief power point in the valley, where worship carries many times more merit than anywhere else in Kathmandu. Stupas and chortens are freestanding Buddhist monuments built to house sacred relics, mark holy places or commemorate events. On one of these walks I was surprised to find huge clumps of marijuana plants growing wild on the side of the road. These plants towered over my head.

Our whole group took a taxi ride to Boudhananth Stupa, which apparently is the central prayer and meeting place of the exiled Tibetan community. There were rows of mounted prayer wheels inscribed with the mantra of compassion: OM MANI PADME HUM (Hail the jewel in the lotus). The Tibetans pronounce it Om Mani Peme Hung. It embodies the compassion and blessing of all the Buddhas and bodhisattvas, particularly of Avalokiteshvara. The Buddha of compassion, Avalokiteshvara is the most important Buddha and karmic deity of Tibet. Pride, jealousy, desire, ignorance, greed and anger are purified and transformed through this mantra. It is also a mantra of protection.

As I walked along the walls the palm of my hand slid from one prayer wheel to another. Spinning each in turn I sent the prayers into the world and beyond. Large piercing eyes were painted on many of the Stupas we went to. The Tibetan Buddhist thankas (religious paintings), hand-held prayer wheels and akshamalas (rosary) were on sale all over Kathmandu.

The time flew by and I found myself sorting my luggage for the trek. Only the bare essentials such as sleeping bag, warm and wet weather gear, survival packets of Earl Grey teabags, M&Ms and other sweets, small towel, basic toiletries, flashlight, first aid kit and lots of toilet rolls were to be packed into the duffel bag provided by the tour organisers. Where we were going there were no toilets, let alone loo paper.

Passports, travel documents and money were to be kept on one's person at all times. During the trek the duffel bags, tents, food and cooking gear were carted by porters and horses. All I had to carry was a small backpack containing a jacket, water bottle, snack and the essential toilet roll in a plastic bag. The rest of my luggage remaining in Kathmandu was locked up with the gear of the other trek members in a storeroom of the hotel.

With great excitement we flew off to Nepalgunj, a town in the south west of Nepal. It was so hot and humid I felt I was wading through the thick air, pushing against a current of sticky treacle. Nepalgunj is an uninspiring place so I was relieved it was only an overnight stay there.

I slept fitfully because my racing mind was filled with thoughts of the adventure to come and a sense of the air attempting to suffocate me. At 4 am the next morning we had breakfast, then flew north for fifty minutes in a small aircraft to Simikot (elevation 2910 meters) in the remote Humla district of Nepal.

Diane admired the flying ability of the pilot, because the runway into Simikot was incredibly short, with a ring of mountains to crash into if you overshot! Flying in and out of there would be hair-raising in inclement weather.

Simikot is a tiny village which has a school and, because of the aircraft landing strip, is the main trading place for the Humli people. There is no other town within many days' walk. As it is nestled in a remote area of rugged mountains, all roads out of Simikot quickly become walking trails.

We had to obtain a special permit to trek through this restricted area where the Humli and Bhotia people live, trading salt and grazing their animals freely on the Tibetan plateau. I was saddened to hear that in recent years a type of pneumonia, brought in by foreigners like myself, had swept through the area and killed about seventy-five people. Harsh conditions and food shortages would have contributed to this disaster.

Lana had an interesting conversation with a western woman working in the area. She told Lana that the increasing felling of the forests had caused severe erosion of the topsoil, depriving it of precious minerals. Apparently, genetically modified rice from the USA was given to the Humli people by the Tibetan government. Unfortunately, the rice was faulty and devoid of any nutrition, thereby exacerbating the problem and making the locals more susceptible to foreign diseases.

We met our friendly porters who doubled as our cooks, and for the first time we camped in tents. I wondered how on earth these small, slightly built men were going to be able to lug all of our camping gear through the mountains. I had the impression that if I gave one of them a bear hug I would crush him. My erected tent seemed so flimsy that I seriously doubted its ability to keep me warm and protect me from the elements.

Our two trekking guides were Sherpas from the Everest region who had been with us since departing Kathmandu. Their job was to oversee everything and set the pace of the trek, making sure no one got lost. I discovered that they were cousins: Ang Gyaltzen Sherpa was twenty-three years old and Karma was a few years older. Both of them had mothers who were the same age as I, so they called me Mum, which I loved.

The trek started for real the next morning when I donned my shorts, hiking boots and pack, then followed the others up the mountain trail into the Himalayas. I soon learned to take Diane's advice to wear a lightweight, ankle-length Indian skirt over my shorts or leggings. This provided some modesty while squatting to relieve myself in the wide open spaces.

From that moment I was in seventh heaven. Don't get me wrong – there were plenty of challenging times for me, but overall I was in my element, Nature, which made my heart sing. The tree-covered mountains in Nepal were spectacular. I breathed in the pristine air, relishing the physicality of spending all the daylight hours hiking up and down mountains while gradually climbing higher and higher towards the Tibetan border.

Mostly we followed Humla Karnali, an icy-cold torrent of a river which roared incessantly over huge, ragged boulders. It was flowing so fast that if you fell in, you would be in India in no time at all! There was plenty of time to stop, meditate and drink in the scenery and enjoy the sunshine. In the distance towering waterfalls tumbled down the slopes below thawing mini glaciers. The fresh smell of the pine forests mingled with

184

that of wild jasmine, which grew everywhere. Butterflies fluttered past, searching for the various little wildflowers that dotted the countryside.

The days took on a natural rhythm, with different people walking ahead with Art and Gyaltzen. Diane mostly stayed at the back of the group encouraging stragglers, while Karma moved back and forth, checking his flock. I often walked on my own in the middle of the group, singing for hours at a time, songs of praise to God and for peace, love and joy in the world. In the quieter times on the flatter paths, I used my prayer beads. Without fail, whenever Lana and I walked together, two eagles would appear in the sky and fly along with us. This occurred day after day, to our elation.

For the first few days a game of musical tenting arrangements ensued, because persons who shall not be named raucously snored their heads off every night! Eventually nocturnal peace was achieved by Melvin and Lana, Diane and Arthur, Yolande and Tracy pairing off respectively. Raju, Michael and I each had our own tent.

The staple diet for vegetarians like myself consisted of potatoes and cabbage ad nauseam. The cooks, to their credit, tried to spice them up and cook them in different ways, but at the end of the day it was still potatoes and cabbage! To be fair, we also had rice or dhal to go with them. I also came to cherish my evening cup of hot chocolate: pure luxury!

All the fresh veggies flown in with us from Kathmandu had become shrivelled and flaccid overnight in the oppressive heat in Nepalgunj, with little of it capable of being resurrected. The cooks had no option but to buy the limited variety of available veggies in Simikot – cabbage and potatoes.

Each day started at 5.30 am with a cup of tea in bed, which

was a sleeping bag on a thin self-inflating mat. A small bowl of hot water was provided to wash the entire body with. Bathing this way is quite an art, and I inadvertently invented a few new yoga postures while perfecting the technique in my tiny tent. I quickly learned that it is definitely best to start with the face and work down the body.

The few moments of relative cleanliness each morning were bliss. Within ten minutes of leaving my tent I was covered in dust and grime again. Keeping myself and my gear clean was impossible. The river was bloody freezing and dangerously fast, so we only bathed in it a couple of times during the whole trek, when we were desperate enough and it was safe enough.

Breakfast was at 7 am. If the weather was fine we ate alfresco, enjoying the million dollar scenery. The meals tent contained a row of battered old metal folding tables with tablecloths, around which we perched on tiny aluminium folding stools. Meal times offered the opportunity for debriefing, airing grievances, sharing lots of jokes, and getting to know each other more fully. Following the evening meal we often had several card games going.

After Michael discovered that I was an ex-dancer we did some partnered ballet stretches and yoga most days before setting off. He admitted that for an old boiler chook I still had a few good moves. On various mornings others of the group joined us in a warm-up while the bemused porters observed us from a safe distance.

I occasionally did some Brain Gym Repatterning with Dr Raju to help his coordination, and for those people needing some extra energy and motivation. I admire and respect the tenacity of Dr Raju, the oldest member of our team. Raju used a pair of hiking sticks to steady himself as he stumbled over the uneven terrain. Showing incredible commitment and courage, by the end of the trek he was so strong and steady on his legs he no longer had need of his sticks. He shared with me that doing the *kora* around Mount Kailash had been a lifelong dream for him.

By 8 am each morning we were trekking. Most days we trekked for eight hours. Some parts were an exhilarating leisurely stroll; others took all of my stamina to put one foot in front of the other and keep going. I found controlling my descent much more challenging for my knees than steep ascents.

There was no way we could be covered for travel insurance on the paths we used. Many times I walked on goat tracks as wide as my shoulders with a sheer wall of rock scraping my right side and a forty foot drop to the Karnali River on my left. As I walked, loose stones beneath my feet tumbled down the cliff face – one slip and it would be all over. In places the only thing to walk on was a felled tree held in place by loose rocks – terrifying to say the least.

No one could afford even a sprained ankle. The only way to get medical aid would be to go all the way back to Simikot on horseback. Fortunately, the only casualties for our group were mild altitude sickness, muscle strain, blistered feet, and varying bouts and intensities of diarrhoea at different times.

Overall, health-wise, I fared better than most. I put it down to the hours spent in gratitude and singing while hiking on my own each day during the trek. The North Americans came well equipped for blisters, with fantastic band aids that were far superior to the useless stuff we Aussies had. Fortunately Michael, Tracy and Art generously shared their supplies with those poor feet in need. Between us all we had a veritable arsenal of vitamins, minerals, colloidal silver and gold, antibiotics, and medicines to fight off bugs.

By mid-morning the porters would zoom effortlessly past us in order to prepare a picnic lunch at the next rest point. After lunch we would set off again, leaving the crew to pack up. Once more they would overtake us with happy cheers so they could set up the tents and prepare dinner for us. The Sherpas and porters were amazingly fit, making the trek look like stroll in the park.

Occasionally we came across men herding goats carrying sacks of salt and sometimes rice on their backs. The weight of the bags, slung either side of the goats' bellies, kept them in place. The nomads were always friendly, and some took the time to sing and dance with Gyaltzen and Karma while another one of them played a wooden flute. In turn Tracy and Michael would sing to them; they both had lovely voices. These light-hearted impromptu concerts with complete strangers happened several times during the twenty-one day trek, providing light relief from the relentless physical grind.

Tracy taught us a song about Mt Kailash by Martin Page, called *The House of Stone and Light*. It had moved Tracy to tears when she first heard it, even though she didn't have a clue where Mt Kailash was at that time. The song played an important part in the synchronicities that led Tracy to go on the trek. I loved the song and it became our theme song, which the whole group regularly sang together:

> Oh Mt Kailash, uncover me
> Come my restoration, wash my body clean
> I've been walking along a crooked path
> Where the walls have fallen
> And broken me in half

188

I'm telling you,
I will not rest until I lay down my head
I'm gonna go in the house of stone and
light
I shall not cry for the blind man I leave
behind
When I go in the house of stone and light,
yeah
In the house of stone and light

Holy Lady show me my soul
Tell me of the place I must surely go
Old man waiting at the gates for me
Give me the wisdom give me the key

… And so on.

At every pass there was a pile of loose stones, prayer flags on poles and dozens of stones with "Om Mani Padme Hum" carved or painted on them. The Sherpas taught us to pick up a stone and throw it on the pile yelling, "Sho! Sho! Sho!" This way our prayers were added to those left by other travellers.

Villages were few and far between. The only way for villagers to get supplies through was on their own backs, on goats, horses, donkeys, or yaks. The most common things being transported were enormous wooden posts and PVC pipes.

*

As we climbed higher the nights grew colder. With the first really cold night I wore practically everything in my pack. On went the thermals, two pairs of socks, tracksuit pants, scarf, gloves, two jumpers and my lap-lap hat, sleeping bag, towel, and anything else not tied down. I looked like a cross between the Michelin Man and a bag lady.

I was secretly terrified of being snap frozen so it took me ages to get to sleep. Fortunately my fears were a major exaggeration of the reality of the situation; however I slept totally rugged up every night just in case. We each had two heat resistant plastic water bottles which were replenished with boiled water every evening in preparation for the next day's hike. They doubled as hot water bottles if only for a few minutes' extra warmth.

I had expected to have some altitude sickness as I have lived all of my life at sea level, but the only times I noticed any trouble was at night when I would wake myself up having to consciously breathe in an extra big breath.

On one of the particularly treacherous paths a horse lost its footing, fell into the river and died. Luckily the courageous men managed save the gear the horse was carrying. Most people in the remote areas of Nepal are really poor, so I was relieved to hear that the owner had horse insurance. No horse would mean no means of livelihood for him. I was glad I didn't see it happen. Lana was particularly distressed about the plight of the horse. I did some Reiki, sent the horse to the light and spent time removing any vibrations of trauma and fear from the rescued gear.

All of Art's clothes and sleeping bag went into the river along with the vials of essences and Chandara's power stick. I wondered to myself: was this mishap a coincidence, or were unseen forces at work endeavouring to sabotage our best efforts by destroying the wand? Fortunately nothing was damaged. When we made camp that night Art spread out his gear on the ground and over his tent to dry. In the morning he had ice-covered, frozen solid clothes. Art held up his stiff-as-a-board jeans, to show me the state they were in.

Over the weeks, strong friendships formed. Michael and Yolande loved talking about their favourite designers such as Gucci, Versace, Calvin Klein and Armani. Michael even had a dream about a Gucci wedding following one of these animated discussions. He gained much pleasure from describing every intricate detail of it to me.

The closest I had come to these clothes was admiring them in magazines. Needless to say, I wasn't in the running for the fashion stakes. I thought I looked cute in my pixyish Tibetan wool hat. Michael would roll his eyes in mock disgust and insist that I stand well away from him every time I wore it. In return for the insult, I jokingly swore to visit him in the good old U.S. of A. at his swanky restaurant with my cap on, and embarrass the hell out of him.

Michael became legendary for his ability to wear a white hat and white tee shirt every day and remain immaculately clean! I seriously considered canonizing him for this ongoing miracle. We all cheered when one day, weeks into the trek, he finally ran out of whites. For the sunny days he wore a wet cotton neck scarf with the knot to one side, silver Dior sunglasses for dressy trekking (black Nikes for when he was feeling sporty), the ever glowing tee shirt, hat, shorts and an umbrella!

Michael made fun of himself wonderfully for us, umbrella held high as he strutted along the path singing. I could vividly see him starring in a movie titled, *Mary Poppins Takes on the Himalayas*. To this day I marvel at how the hell he managed to squeeze an umbrella into his duffel bag.

Tracy, Michael and Yolande got on like a house on fire and could often be found laughing raucously together in the shelter of a tent. Humour kept us together and motivated the strugglers to keep going.

Practical jokes abounded. One night Melvin hid under a sleeping bag in Yolande and Tracy's tent. As they entered the dark tent Melvin let out a huge roar and pounced on them. The girls of course got a hell of a fright, but so did Melvin when Tracy beat him to a pulp. He didn't try that prank again.

Bite me and *Eat me* were slang terms that hadn't hit Australia yet. We teased the Yanks a lot about their use. Melvin gave Yolande a huge hug one morning while surreptitiously putting a huge "Eat Me" sign on her back. She wore it for most of the day before discovering it. Yolande got her own back by hiding Mel's sleeping bag. A night without a sleeping bag is not a great experience in these cold conditions. Mel complained to Lana about the unfairness of it all. "What the hell do you expect with all your childish antics?" said Lana pragmatically.

*

For Lana, Yolande and Melvin, ongoing diarrhoea sapped their strength and took the joy out of the climb. Tracy also had two bouts of severe dysentery with hours of vomiting. Remembering how weak and shaky I felt in India, I couldn't begin to imagine what it would be like to feel as I did then and hike all day, every day! I only had the runs for a few days, and they were the hardest days of the trek for me.

Meanwhile, Art and Diane were not having an easy time of it. On a couple of nights when the going got tough, Diane would share my tent. Deep personal challenges were occurring, and they were both experiencing conflict. I was relieved that this trip was not challenging at all on inner levels, as India had been for me.

192

As we climbed higher the vegetation thinned out. Gradually the trees disappeared and were replaced by grasslands, then by bare stones and slippery shale. The relentless wind whipped up the dust from the bleak mountains. My nose, teeth and tongue became caked in powder-fine grit, as was every square inch of me. The grey dust settled in my hair and dried out my face. On a good day I looked a hundred years old. When I smiled my face cracked, exposing every wrinkle and fine line I possessed. I wrapped a scarf around my face in an attempt to filter the air, but, combined with the effort of climbing at ever higher altitudes, this made breathing difficult.

Curiously, when Lana and I walked together, I often would lose my footing and be unsteady on my feet. It was as if an invisible gremlin was pushing me off balance. This happened so often that Lana noticed it and commented on it. On one occasion we were descending some particularly slippery, steep switch-backs. I skated and scrambled along on the loose stones. It felt as if a malevolent force was holding me by the seat of my pants and shoving me around. I picked up speed as I was propelled forward out of control.

"Look out, Patti!" Lana yelled as I sped past her. I hurtled headlong towards a precipice. My arms flailed the air helplessly as I attempted to slow my descent. In desperation I slid to the ground like a baseball player going for second base. I screeched to a dusty stop with my feet hanging in thin air over the edge of the cliff. Phew, that was a close one!

"Are you okay, Patti?" asked Lana with concern as she sat down in the dirt next to me. She held my arms as if I might suddenly fly off the edge unannounced.

After this incident I watched the ground like a hawk and chose always to walk in front of Lana, as this way I was steadier on my feet. Once Lana called out to me, but I didn't catch what she said. I kept walking as I turned and looked up to ask, "What?" Whack! I smacked into a low tree branch and was thrown onto my backside with the force of the impact. There were fewer trees in this area and I wasn't expecting a visit from one. With my cap on and constantly looking down for a good footing, I hadn't seen the tree let alone the branch. My head spun with mild concussion.

"What did you say?" I asked, nursing my throbbing head.

Lana fell about laughing and clutching her stomach. When she finally came up for air she wheezed, "I said, 'Duck!'" She rolled around heh, heh, hehing her unique laugh for several minutes, then yelled, "DUCK!" again and collapsed into more peals of laughter.

As you can see, we were pretty easily entertained. My head ached all day, and a large bump came up on my forehead. Apart from my bruised pride I was fine.

*

At a village near the Tibetan border the poverty was depressing. In these harsh, freezing conditions children walked barefoot. The few flimsy clothes they had were in tatters, with the pattern and colour of the material faded beyond recognition.

Just inside one village I rested and had a drink from my water bottle. A beautiful, open-faced young Humla woman squatted down next to me and started talking and gesticulating towards a little two-year-old girl. I turned to Gyaltzen who was sitting near me and asked him to interpret what she had said. He

194

was very embarrassed, and hesitated with his translation. This young mother was asking me to adopt her daughter and take her with me back to Australia.

It was distressing to think that this child's opportunities in life were so limited that the mother would rather give her to a stranger to take away forever than watch her endure life there with her. My mind raced analysing the logistics of honouring such a request and finally I realized the futility of it. I didn't know what to say.

As we continued to trek over the increasingly desolate mountains, Tibet was tantalizingly close. The relentless climb up to Nara La Pass, the highest point we traversed in Nepal, was a killer. Michael found that day particularly hard going as he had spent all the previous night vomiting.

The border seemed endlessly always just over the next peak, until finally there Tibet was! A spontaneous celebration erupted as we looked down to the river and across to the Chinese checkpoint high on the other side. We whooped and hollered, sang and danced around with the porters. High above us an eagle circled, observing our antics. We would cross the border with the two Sherpas, leaving the porters in Nepal. The plan was to drive to and from Mount Kailash, then rejoin the porters at the border and trek back to Simikot.

*

The border checkpoint was a tiny building in the middle of nowhere, where we waited for a few hours for officials to arrive. Our baggage was thoroughly checked for contraband, and especially for photos of the Dalai Lama. Diane had warned us that one photo of his Holiness could be cause for the whole group being turned back and refused entry.

The border official's manner was terse and unsmiling as he checked over our passports, visas and permits. Finally we were all cleared, and we piled into two jeeps with official Chinese government drivers. The drivers had absolutely no interest in getting to know us better, treating our group with quiet disdain. The Chinese pop music on the radio was interesting, though, and we had fun sing-songing along with it.

Lana and I both spontaneously burst into tears of joy at the realization that we were actually in Tibet! I was inexplicably ecstatic. We cried and laughed uncontrollably for ten full minutes. Through the tears Lana said, "I don't know what's got into me. I'm not usually this emotional!"

Prior to arriving in Taklakot we visited our first monastery inside Tibet. Monks greeted us at the doors of the monastery and offered us small metal cups of yak butter tea. It was very rich tasting and I was unable to finish it. We were then ushered through ancient thick carved wooden doors into a temple. Statues of Buddha and colourful thankas lined the walls. The only lighting was from oil lamps and candles. A thick musty smell of age, earthen walls and incense filled my nostrils and transported me back in time. To my right in the dim light were the sacred texts stored in their wooden pigeon holes. I sat and meditated for quite a while in this sanctuary.

One of the great halls we were guided through was empty save for one lone shrine to Maitreya, the future Buddha. We turned the lines of prayer wheels, then we thanked the monks and headed for Taklakot.

This was a mere shadow of what the monastery had been like prior to the Chinese invasion. The Chinese had ransacked all the monasteries in the area and killed most of the monks. What we saw were treasures that had been hidden from the Chinese. In very recent times some of the monasteries have been permitted to operate with the strictest government scrutiny.

As I left the monastery a strange thing happened. My face and neck broke out in red angry blotches and welts, as if I had been burned. It didn't hurt and it wasn't itchy. In fact it was Diane who alerted me to it when she pulled on my arm to stop me and said, "Oh my God! What happened to your face?" When we were settled into our quarters at Taklakot I put some cream on my face, but it didn't make any difference. I wasn't particularly worried as there were no mirrors to distress myself with and I just thought the incessant wind had caused a reaction on my sensitive skin. Someone gave me lavender oil to soothe it, but apparently I still looked awful.

Diane became increasingly distressed about my condition and insisted that we do some Kinesiology muscle checking to find out what had caused it. We discovered that it was related to a past life that Diane needed to remember, which was why she was reacting to my plight.

It transpired that Diane and I knew each other in a Tibetan lifetime where we were both males. According to Diane, she was jealous of my influence and popularity as a monk so she put acid on my face, tortured me to death, then threw my body off a mountain slope which covered me in a landslide of scree.

After remembering this lifetime Diane forgave herself and I forgave her and healed the trauma from my body and energy field. Apparently visiting the monastery had triggered my cellular memory in a very literal manner. I was surprised that I had experienced no emotional reactivity to Diane's story.

Years ago I had accessed a past life memory of being a Tibetan Buddhist monk, carefully rewriting the sacred texts and storing them for posterity in small alcoves. In that lifetime I was quite disciplined in a high-principled, rigid sort of way. Diane had just provided another part of the story from that same life. The next morning my face was significantly better and rapidly healed. Diane was again comfortable around me.

Taklakot was a "real" town inside the Chinese border with electricity (occasionally), cars and shops, where we slept in beds for the first time since leaving Nepalgunj. Our quarters were derelict ex-army barracks converted into a spartan guest house of sorts.

To have a meal with fresh vegetables and rice was heaven. We were able to replenish our supplies of treats, which were essential for morale boosting. I still had the bag of M&Ms saved for a real emergency, though – things hadn't been that desperate yet.

Loudhailers lined the streets, blaring out constant streams of Chinese propaganda. All the buildings in Taklakot were in disrepair and filthy. Through the decay I could see that this had once been a much larger, thriving place. This unloved town was full of prostitutes and bored, disgruntled border guards. Very few Tibetans were seen.

An enormous glass greenhouse, once the pride of the place, was empty, broken, and falling down. Growing anything here would be a challenge, so I couldn't understand the neglect of the greenhouse. To grow a few trees required six-foot walls of rocks to protect them from the relentless wind.

I thought India had the worst toilets I had ever seen. I was in for a shock. There was a fifty-meter walk from my room to the toilet, which consisted of a rough cubicle with a hole in the wafer-thin boarding floor, which I prayed would hold my weight. While I was relieving myself, I heard a noise below me so I interrupted what I was doing to peer down into the hole. The toilet was perched on the side of a hill, with pigs and dogs feeding on the fresh offerings falling from the heavens! Give me a mountain trail anytime.

*

Upon seeing the bleak, stony landscape we passed through on our way to Darchan, I was grateful we were driving rather than walking for that section. On the way we traversed an expansive plain devoid of any vegetation. There in the middle of nowhere was a single tent and boom gate. I thought it was hysterical to have a gate to stop traffic when there were no roads, let alone fences to direct people there! It was like a veritable dunny on a heath. In the distance to the left and right of us, we could see Tibetan pilgrims in trucks and on foot creating their own routes to Darchan.

On our right some magnificent mountains came into view. I turned to Michael and said, "God! What do you think of that mountain?" The mountain turned out to be Mount Mandhata (7728 metres), and at that time only a French expedition had explored it. It felt vibrant and alive. Michael and I seemed to be the only two of our group significantly impressed by its energy. Everyone else was holding out for their first glimpse of the more revered Mt Kailash.

Heading north we passed between two large lakes. The left one, Lake Rakshas Tal, was apparently devoid of life because of the souls of hundreds of spirits trapped beneath it. Even from the jeep, the vibration of Rakshas Tal was totally different from the religiously significant Lake Manasarovar to our right. It did indeed look and feel less alive.

At Darchan we pitched our tents amongst the rapidly increasing number of pilgrims pouring in from India and all over Tibet in anticipation of the Saga Dawa Festival. That afternoon I immersed myself in Tibetan culture, admiring the chunky jewellery and thick yak fur-lined coats and hats of the pilgrims, and exploring the tents of the traders. I bought some prayer flags and a large picture of Maitreya Buddha printed on cloth and framed with brightly-coloured brocade.

Often pilgrims stopped me to ask if I had any photographs of the Dalai Lama. I would have loved to oblige them if smuggling a photo in didn't mean consequences for our whole group.

Very light snow fell all the day of the Saga Dawa Festival, which is the annual pole-raising ceremony held by the Tibetan Buddhists to renew the spirit of the people and carry their prayers into the New Year. It is held each year on Buddha's birthday, the full moon day during the Tibetan month of May/June. This was a magical day and one of the highlights of my trip.

The pole is huge – about fifty feet tall – and absolutely covered in strings of multi-coloured prayer flags. Everyone walked endlessly around and around it, going clockwise, praying and throwing into the air handfuls of coloured paper squares with prayers written on them. The ground rapidly became a bright carpet of prayers upon the light layer of snow. I added my string of prayer flags to the pole as I prayed for peace and happiness for all the people of the world, and health and harmony for Gaia. Around the perimeter huge piles of incense were being burned. Ever so slowly the pole was painstakingly moved from horizontal to vertical as the prayers continued incessantly.

From time to time Chinese propaganda would blare out on loudspeakers in an attempt to disrupt the rituals and celebrations. Overall I had a sense of duty rather than

200

malice from the Chinese armed guards, who chose to play the speeches in the breaks rather than drowning out the ceremonies. There were two other western groups there. I don't know how much our collective presence toned down the Chinese government's interference.

The haunting low drones of the High Lama's long horns rang through the crisp air. When they combined with the short horns, cymbals, bells, drums (*damaru*) and chanting of the other monks, my whole body tingled. A child monk recognized as having had a previous life as a High Lama was given the privilege of blowing the conch shell. These sounds seemed to blast a clear path before the monks as they led a procession around the pole. Their religious artefacts, ceremonial hats and robes created quite a spectacle.

As the hours of prayer accumulated, the intensity and expectation of the crowd grew to fever pitch. Finally the pole was almost vertical and the pilgrims formed an expectant circle around it. A great cheer erupted as the pole was put in place. It was auspicious that the pole was perfectly straight – a good omen for the coming year.

*

That evening was the time for the planetary alignment and link-up with Chandara and others around the world. The Stargate meditation just before mealtime went gracefully and smoothly, with Diane guiding us through what Chandara had written:

> In preparation for the Stargate meditation, please align and centre your energies, your focus and your concentration within your physical body. Loosely shake or relax the physical body releasing any tension you may be experiencing.

201

Let us begin by focusing your concentration and energy at the belly, the Hara.

Place your left hand with the palm over the belly and begin taking a deep breath. Inhale through the nose, exhale thru the mouth, blowing the breath all the way out from the Hara.

'Do three breaths: Inhaling through the nose - filling the lungs completely with air.

Breathe out through the mouth, pushing all the air from the lungs and the diaphragm, and centre your energy at the Hara.

Align and balance your focus and Centre.

Begin moving the energy and focus from the Hara up through the torso on your right side.

Move through the chest, up into the right shoulder, down the right arm, through the elbow, the wrist and out the crystal in the palm of the right hand.

As you move this energy you may choose to ask that all the frequencies, energy blockages and things you no longer need in your life to be moved through this channel and out the crystal in the palm of your right hand.

Now picture the etheric grids of the Earth, which are found surrounding the Earth in the high atmosphere above the planet. Concentrate on the Christ Consciousness grid or the Planetary Ascension grid. Which ever you choose is the correct one for you. You can do this using intention; your thoughts will make the connection for you.

Now move the energy out through the right palm crystal and up into the grid. Ask for the connection to be made and ask that any frequencies you no longer need be sent to this grid to be transmuted in perfection and returned to the light as one.

Now focus on the grid, slowly moving across the grid from right to left, transmuting the energies into perfect energy. You may now ask to connect this energy from the grid down into your left palm, connecting with the Palm Crystal of the crystalline light body.

As you bring this perfect energy down from the grid, through all the layers of the Earth and into the crystal of your left palm, you are replenishing your light body and physical form with all the energies and frequencies that you need in your life.

Now bring the energy from the grid through the left palm crystal, through the arm down the torso on the left side and back to the Hara.....

The meditation continued in this vein, with the circling energy going from the Hara, out the right palm to the grid, and coming back down from the grid into the left palm. It cleansed and regenerated as it was breathed through us.

This process was repeated flowing from the Hara, down the right leg to the centre of the Earth and back up the left leg to the Hara. Finally a figure eight energy flow was created between the grid around the planet and the centre of the Earth through the Hara centre of our bodies. Diane completed the process with a short prayer.

I was pleased that Chandara, like me, saw people as human crystals: crystalline light bodies with the ability to take on and amplify light energies.

Art had not used Chandara's wand and essences in the Stargate meditation, as she had suggested. I was beginning to be concerned that Art was not holding to his agreement to Chandara, Diane and me. Afterwards I asked Art, "Have you placed the essences in the river?"

"No, it hasn't felt right yet. Leave it to me. I'll wait for guidance on it," Art replied.

*

Michael and I compared what we were receiving in our meditations and found we were in agreement on almost everything. The four directions information that Tracy contributed related to the four main landmarks: Mount Kailash in the north, Mt Mandhata in the south, Lake Rakshas Tal to the west and Lake Manasarovar in the east. Michael saw the polarity that we were working with more as light and dark energies than masculine/feminine, as I saw it. We both received instructions to clear the trapped spirits from under Lake Rakshas Tal and take steps towards healing the energetic polarity imbalance.

When I tuned into Mt Kailash a few days earlier, the male energy of the mountain warned me it couldn't change very fast. As Michael and I discussed the idea of doing this clearing meditation with Art, Tracy and Diane, Art began behaving strangely. He agreed it was a good idea, all the while becoming more and more agitated. We suggested that Art represent Mt Kailash in the north and Diane represent Lake Rakshas Tal in the west. Tracy volunteered to be Lake Manasarovar in the east. Michael was very definite that he needed to be the centre-point, representing both the masculine and feminine principle and the conduit through which the energies would travel. As I had an affinity with Mt Mandhata I was selected for the south position. Although it was a bitterly cold night, Art insisted that we do the meditation outside where we could see Mt Kailash, and he set off to mark out the ground for the ceremony.

The rest of the group were notified of our intentions and invited to join us if it felt appropriate. Melvin came to me and admitted he didn't understand or necessarily relate to

204

what we were trying to do but he wanted to join in and send love to the situation. I thought that was great, and found his integrity and honesty refreshing.

Lana, Yolande, Mel and Raju took places in the gaps of the diamond shape formed by the people at the four nodal points. Rugged up in our full snow gear, all eight of us took off our gloves and held hands. Michael took position in the centre. He called upon the highest of divine light beings in service to humanity and the Earth's spiritual evolvement to be present. We individually called upon personal guides and protectors according to our varying faiths. I sent love down to Gaia, the consciousness of the Earth, and up to the Great Central Sun. Energy poured down through the top of my head and up through the soles of my feet.

We then turned our attention to Lake Rakshas Tal and asked for permission to free the trapped souls from beneath the lake. As one unit we drew upon the support of the light beings enfolding us.

Everyone focused their energy on Diane to give her strength to do what was required. Unfortunately, there was no palpable energy coming from Art to support Diane. At one point she sank to the ground exhausted, literally wilting with the effort of it all, then rallied and stood tall again. We all intensified our efforts.

With a huge upsweeping rush I felt the trapped souls being freed en mass and sent to the light. Diane did an amazing job holding the energy of Lake Rakshas Tal throughout this whole process. On our behalf, Michael thanked the light beings and closed the ceremony.

It was far too cold to hang around and talk, so we scurried back to the relative warmth of our tents. It had been a wonderful, empowering day with the pole raising ceremony, planetary alignment and freeing the souls under Lake Rakshas Tal.

Before breakfast the next morning I gave Michael a Touch for Health balance as he was feeling out of sorts and had a squirbly stomach. He put it down to having to anchor the energy as the centre point in the previous night's process. We were on our own, so I felt free to ask him how he thought the meditation went. He sucked in his breath and hesitated searching for the most diplomatic reply, so I went first, sharing what I was thinking.

"I think Art was actively trying to block what we were endeavouring to do, and Diane did a great job holding the energy under those circumstances. However, I am sure the freeing of the souls was complete."

"Yes, that's what I felt, too," agreed Michael.

Michael told me of his decision to stay at Lake Manasarovar instead of doing the *kora* around Mt Kailash. The lake had more of a pull for him, and Michael wanted to be on his own to continue working on the inner levels free from outside interference. I thought that was a great idea.

*

That morning we were set to begin a three-day journey around Mt Kailash. The snow had increased concerns regarding the group's safety during the *kora*, and a long discussion ensued. It was impressed upon us the importance of reaching our target camping spot each night. Blizzards were known to spring up without warning. The previous week a group had done the *kora* while it was knee deep in snow. A Frenchman from that group broke his leg and was airlifted out by helicopter.

As tour organisers, Art and Diane were initially not happy with the idea of Michael going off on his own to Lake Manasarovar. Dr Raju opted at the last minute to stay at the guesthouse at Darchan as he was concerned about his health. Several of us were secretly relieved, as Raju was the oldest in our group, and he was finding the altitude a strain. We would be going over Dolma La pass at 5630 metres, which would be challenging for all of us. Three of us had experienced warning dreams of someone being severely injured or killed while doing the *kora*. After lots of negotiation via the Sherpas, and extra money paid by Michael and Raju to the drivers, permission was granted for the two to stay behind.

An agreement between India and China allows several hundred Jains, Buddhists and Hindus to make the nine day pilgrimage to Lake Manasarovar and do the *parikrama* around Mt. Kailash each year. All three religions go clockwise around Mt Kailash. The Bon Pos, a pre-Buddhist religion, travel anticlockwise, so we were constantly passing them on our journey.

Karma literally means "action" and is the natural law of cause and effect. It means that whatever we do with our body, speech or mind will have a corresponding result. This applies to positive loving actions as well as negative hurtful actions. The results of *karma* are often delayed into future lives.

Buddha said, "Do not overlook negative actions merely because they are small; however small a spark may be, it can burn down a haystack as big as a mountain. Do not overlook tiny good actions thinking they are of no benefit; even tiny drops of water in the end fill a huge vessel." In relation to karma the Dalai Lama says, "If you try to subdue your selfish motives – anger and so forth – and develop more kindness and compassion for others, ultimately you yourself would benefit more than you would otherwise. So sometimes I say that the wise selfish person should practice this way. Foolish selfish people are always thinking of themselves, and the result is negative. Wise selfish people think of others, help others as much as they can, and the result is that they too receive benefit."

The most pious of each of the religions prostrate themselves along the ground on their bellies, walk two steps, pray, kneel, then stretch out along the ground again. They wear tough leather aprons and padded mitts on their hands, a little like the flat gloves that boxers punch into, to protect them from the snow, ice and rocks. It takes twenty-one days to caterpillar walk the fifty-two kilometre circuit like this. Others walk the *kora* in a single day! Diane told us about an inner *kora* that passes the two lakes to the south of Mt. Kailash. Only those that have done thirteen circumambulations of Mt. Kailash may follow this route.

The first day went fairly routinely, apart from my having mild diarrhoea and tummy pains. To the left of the path at Shiva-tsal (elevation 5390 m) Gyaltzen showed us where an article of clothing or a drop of blood was offered to Mt. Kailash by pilgrims as a symbol of leaving the past behind. One side of the hill was littered with clothes in varying states of disrepair, like an eerie graveyard.

In places we had to cross small streams covered in ice. I was glad that the ice held my weight, because hiking with saturated clothes in these freezing conditions would not have been at all helpful.

All the monasteries on the *kora* circuit were destroyed by the Chinese. Only one, Nyanri Gompa, had been reopened. It was perched on a hill to our left, like an eagle's aerie. It

208

seemed to be half built, half carved out of the rock. Inside it was very dark and mysterious with tiny rooms and alcoves with altars.

A lot of thought from each of us had gone into what to give up to the mountain at Dolma La Pass. Tradition demanded that you release or give up something you hold dear to your heart as a spiritual cleansing. I had brought with me the red tail feather of a black cockatoo, which Tony had given me just before he died. For several days I had received in meditation that I needed to give the feather to Lana at Dolma La Pass. The pass is the highest point of the *kora* and the highest point of the whole trek. Huge piles of accumulated red, green, blue, yellow and white prayer flags were spread over the ground with fresh snow upon them.

I went over to Lana and explained the significance of the feather to me personally, and how to Aboriginal people these cockatoos represent the spirits of their ancestors. When I offered it to her, Lana was surprised and happy because for days she had been feeling that it was important to give me her Maori Greenstone necklace, which had been in her family for generations. We cried as we hugged each other, knowing that both gifts would be respected by their new keepers.

Melvin asked me to cut his shoulder-length hair short as a way of releasing the last seven years of his life and starting afresh. He tied his pieces of cropped hair to the prayer flags. We did a group meditation and sang to Mount Kailash, then continued on our way.

The second day of the *kora* was the toughest one of the whole journey for me. Lana and Yolande strode out at a relentless cracking pace which was a struggle to keep up with. Surprisingly, this was their way of getting the day over and done with. By now both of them were past exhaustion point and running on raw adrenaline, like automatons. The torturous day proved to be a twelve-hour forced march with very short rests.

At one point Art joined me as we scrambled over the rocks. He finally admitted that he hadn't resonated with the ceremony of the other night, and that he had actively blocked what we were doing. I asked, "Why didn't you say so straight away when we first discussed it? It would have been more in integrity to be honest with us and choose to not participate!" Art was either not willing or not able to give me a reason, and he strode off ahead of me without replying.

That evening we all crawled exhausted into our sleeping bags inside a small, single-roomed earthen shelter. The fine dust from the walls was suffocating so we left the door slightly ajar in spite of the cold.

The third day of the *kora* was a breeze by comparison. The two jeeps ready to take us to Lake Manasarovar, were a welcome sight at day's end.

Bathing in the lake and meditating there is supposed to heal seven generations before you and seven generations into the future. Needless to say it was absolute brass monkey conditions in the water – that's devotion to the family for you. I bathed in the lake, allowing the chill of the water to penetrate to my bones and cleanse me, then I sat cross-legged at the water's edge and meditated.

Later that day Michael, Diane and I met on a small hill from which we had a view of both lakes, Mt Kailash and Mt Mandhata. I shared with them what Art had said. We did a final healing and clearing meditation in this central position and activated a beautiful crystal from Canada, which Diane offered up to that place. During that meditation I was

210

reminded that the spirit of Mt. Kailash had warned me it wouldn't/couldn't change too rapidly. I realized that I was being too harsh on Art. As representative of Mt Kailash in the meditation, Art was only reflecting the energy of the mountain that I had perceived earlier. We had all embarked on this journey with the highest and best intentions; and everything has its own divine timing.

*

Joy! Oh! Joy! We were told about some hot springs nearby. In a flash we were ready to go and have our first proper cleanup in hot water in weeks. The smell of sulphur was really strong as I stepped out of the jeep and gazed over the unattractive desolate landscape. The roughly built concrete bathing house visually left a lot to be desired. Lana, Diane, Yolande and I squeezed together into the cement trough doubling as a bath, sighing with ecstasy as the hot sulphur water washed away our aches and pains. The minerals in the water rejuvenated my parched face so that I almost looked myself again.

We rested for two days at Lake Manasarovar before starting our homeward journey. Mel, Yolande and Lana had been the most incapacitated with illness, which made trekking unattractive to them. Much discussion with the Sherpas and Diane ensued, to see if there was another way, preferably in jeeps, to go back to Kathmandu. Unfortunately they finally had no option but to trek back over the Himalayas with the rest of us. I personally was looking forward to trekking the home journey.

Fresh provisions were bought in Taklakot, then the whole group enjoyed a delicious meal at the only restaurant in town. When I arrived back at the Nepalese border I stopped, gave thanks and meditated before crossing into.Nepal. What a powerful experience on many levels Tibet had been for me!

After dinner that night I asked Art, "Have you put the Star Essences into the waters?"

He replied, "No."

Now it was too late as we were back in Nepal. It was his responsibility, so I let the matter drop.

The mountains closest to the border were the most challenging physically. A few days into the return trek, Yolande collapsed with exhaustion, unable to go another step. She was totally depleted on all levels. Gear was taken off one of the horses and shared between the Sherpas and porters so that Yolande could ride for a while. Given a chance to rest on horseback as we travelled, Yolande regained her strength, and the next day she was able to walk again.

Lana was not a happy woman either. She was irritated all over. "I shoved Mel awake last night because something was running over my legs in my sleeping bag. I got him to shine the torch on me and we searched through my sleeping gear but found nothing. Zilch! Something is bugging me though; I feel like my skin is crawling," she explained, showing me the red lumps all over her hands and calves.

Actually, it was crawling! Diane, Lana, Tracy and Melvin all contracted scabies during the trek. I guess it was inevitable that some of us would contract scabies, as we were continually covered in dust and our gear was put on the dirt when the porters had rests on the trek. Fortunately, when they were back in their homes, it took only one treatment of medication and they were cured.

We camped one night outside a Nepalese Buddhist monastery. The young head monk was very welcoming, and proudly showed us all the farming, reforestation and educational

212

projects underway. There was a good variety of healthy-looking fruit trees and vegetables being cultivated with sponsorship from overseas people. I enjoyed sitting quietly in the prayer hall while the young monks were reading from the sacred texts, praying and meditating. I soaked up all the sights, sounds and smells, and the interactions of the teenage monks just being themselves. This insight into daily life at the monastery was worth a dozen books on the subject.

Another treat was in store for us near the monastery if we were prepared for the hike. To some, the word "hike" didn't sound at all inviting at the end of a long day, but to me the lure of a thermal spring waterfall to bathe in was well worth a little extra effort. I gathered together the remaining shreds of my energy and a few of us scrambled quite a long way up a rocky gorge. Just when I was thinking we would never find it and that I was too tired to walk back, we were there. Showering under a hot waterfall in the wide open spaces in the mountains of Nepal was a delicious peak experience.

The return journey took on a pleasant rhythm for me and I continued to have a good time. Finally we arrived back at Simikot, where inclement cloudy weather awaited us. I couldn't believe the trek was over. There was a delay with our flight as the dense cloud cover made it impossible for a plane to land safely. On that short runway there was no room for error. The next day the flight was also cancelled.

An impromptu beauty parlour was created in the meals tent in an attempt to allay the boredom of waiting. We did manicures and pedicures for each other and created a few new hairstyles. Yolande insisted on plucking Lana's generous free-range eyebrows for her. As there was nothing else to do, a few of the men joined in and we preened each other for hours like lounging monkeys. Nevertheless, concern crept into our group, as we all needed to be back in Kathmandu by certain days to catch connecting flights home. We did prayers and meditations to clear the weather. This didn't work, so we kept investigating why this delay was happening.

Several members of our group were at important crossroads in their lives. Decisions needed to be made soon after returning home, creating unconscious fear and uncertainty. I led a group clearing of these fears, and we restored our faith in divine guidance and trust in ourselves that we would make wise beneficial decisions. Within two hours the weather cleared and a flight was arranged.

*

It was sad to say goodbye to everyone, as we had been through such magic and potent experiences together. My life was touched in a positive way by each one of the members of our group. Over recent years, Diane has led five groups into Tibet. Two years after the trek that I went on, Diane was happy to report to me that Lake Rakshas Tal now has fish in it. It is noticeably more alive! Hopefully our efforts have, in part, contributed to this improvement of the lake.

I continued from Kathmandu to Toronto to give a presentation at the annual International Educational Kinesiology Gathering. From there I went to London and had a joyful reunion with my niece Katie, who was nursing there. She showed me the sights of London, then I caught the train to Kings Lynn to visit Tony's daughter Amanda.

Amanda's teenage kids, Aaron, Chez and Nicholas, were good fun. We danced and larked about in the village square one evening to a lively Mungo Jerry concert. What a blast from the past! The five of us piled into Amanda's car and drove to Wiltshire. We slept under the stars on the full moon equinox on Silbury Hill along with druids, crop circle buffs and Wiccans. Unfortunately no new crop circles were created overnight. All around the hill were the remains of old crop circles, though.

We went to Stonehenge, Avebury, Glastonbury and Challis Well Gardens, to name just a few of the power places we visited. What an amazing area! Before I could blink, it was time to return to London and fly home to Perth.

I'll Send You a Good Man

Two years had passed since Tony had died. He continued to visit me and my closest friends from time to time. I'd be driving my car when he would materialize in the back, leaning forward and propping his elbows on the front bucket seats. "Hello Sugar Plum," he'd say. Only it came out sounding more like Sugar Ppp-lerrm as he stuck out his tongue and used an exaggerated fake French accent. This silly term of endearment always made me smile. Having a man in my life was not on the agenda. Celibacy was comfortable while I was healing, but after two years I slowly began to thaw.

I was invited by a German friend, Henning, to go for a sail on his yacht, My Toy. I have always loved sailing so I jumped at that chance. What a perfect summer's day! Not a cloud in the azure sky and just enough wind to take the two of us out to sea. Henning lowered me off the back of the yacht and I held onto an inflated rubber tube attached to a rope. As I skurfed along I pushed aside the thought that I would make lovely juicy shark bait trawling along in the water like that. The cool of the water was refreshing, and I was soon carefree.

After a swim we relaxed and, as we ate our picnic lunch, chatted about Henning's plans to sail around the world. Out of nowhere appeared a huge cloud of orange and black monarch butterflies: dozens and dozens of them. We were two miles out to sea with not another boat in sight.

"For goodness sake! Where did they come from?"

Ever practical, Henning replied, "They've been blown out to sea by the easterly wind."

"This is special, Henning!"

"I'm sure it happens fairly often," he countered.

I couldn't quite believe that this was a commonplace event, especially not in these numbers. Butterflies covered the sails and danced around Henning and me. They decorated our hair and arms, and two landed on my nose.

"Henning, the butterflies are telling me my love is thinking of me. This means I'm going to meet a new partner within two months," I beamed.

Henning looked at me as though I had completely lost my mind. "Patti, the wind has just blown them out to sea."

Ignoring his disbelief I repeated myself: "I bet you that I'm going to meet a new man within the next two months." It was obvious we weren't going to change each other's point of view, so we just sat and enjoyed our visitors.

Once I was back on dry land again I telephoned Diane. "Diane, do you remember when that mass of butterflies flew around me in the bush and told me that I was going to meet a man in two months? You know, before I met Tony?"

"Yeah. Why?"

"It happened again while I was sailing with Henning. There were more than thirty of them. I've never seen anything like that out to sea! They were monarchs, too."

"Yahoo, Patti! What do you think it means?"

"I'm going to meet someone special soon. I can feel it in my bones."

"Oh, I'm so happy for you!" said Diane, never doubting. It was great to talk to a good mate who understood me.

In mid January, the same summer, I became obsessed with learning Latin dancing and particularly tango. I asked around and found out about beginner's classes in a café in Claremont, an up-market suburb of Perth.

I mentioned tango to Diane and Susie and both expressed interest. Diane and I agreed to rendezvous at the café one Tuesday night, as she was going to meet a man there who wanted to buy some vertical blinds from her. This man, Raoul, turned out to be South American. With him was an Argentinean in his early fifties called Roberto. We briefly introduced ourselves, then the tango class started.

By the end of the first lesson I was hooked. As there was a shortage of men we roped in Diane's brother Melvin. It is actually quite hard to dance tango well, especially for the average red-blooded Australian female. The man leads one hundred percent, which means the female follows passively one hundred percent. That was hard for me to do initially; well, actually it still is! I kept trying to guess what the man wanted, pre-empting him, which frustrated both of us. If the man goes blank or is unsure of what to do next, the woman just has to pause and do nothing until he decides his next move. Patience was never one of my virtues, and my mind would race with all the steps I would love to do to the music if I was leading! It took about twelve months to break me in.

Susie and Diane came to class for about a month, then decided tango wasn't for them. Melvin unfortunately lasted only three lessons before he put it in the too-hard basket. Roberto the Argentinean continued with the tango class. We were encouraged to rotate partners to give us more experience, and to be fair to people like me who hadn't come with one.

Roberto and I would chat in the breaks, and over time he seemed to express an interest in me. I had decided already that he was way too conventional for me: we were chalk and cheese. I abstained from alcohol and was vegetarian, and he was a major meat eater who always had wine with the evening meal. Australians can't compare with the meat-eating capabilities of Argentineans. An Argentine barbecue is like a work of art when you compare it to the overcooked Australian version. My logic told me we were incompatible. He knew nothing of meditation, and the possibility of reincarnation had never crossed his Catholic mind.

The more we talked, the more convinced I was that he didn't have a hope in hell of being my partner. The clincher was when he told me he was recovering from sixty-one sessions of radiation treatments for throat cancer. Emotionally, I headed for the hills. I needed that kind of man like I needed a hole in the head! If that wasn't enough, he also had an enlarged heart and arrhythmia, a result of rheumatic fever as a child, which required him to have heart surgery to repair a damaged valve.

In spite of all this information I had to admit I liked him; and over the months of tango lessons I warmed more and more to him. He was always very sweet and gentlemanly with me. I would talk at length to Susie about Roberto and why he wasn't suited

219

to me. She gave me a wry smile and said, "Gee, for a guy you're not at all interested in, you sure talk about him a lot."

That pulled me up short. Susie was right: Roberto was frequently on my mind and in my conversations. Mostly I thought about how the butterflies must have gotten it wrong, and that this was a sick cosmic joke on me. Falling in love with a man who might die soon was too painful to contemplate. Once in a life was enough.

Five months of tango lessons turned Roberto into a competent dancer, but whenever he danced with me he couldn't think straight and would have two left feet. "I'm sorry, Patti. I want to impress you so much that I mess up when we dance together," Roberto said as he gingerly lifted his foot off my crunched toes.

"Why don't you relax; you've already done that."

I smiled at his surprised expression. The ice maiden was melting.

We had our first official date at his place. The sweetie had gone to much trouble, chasing up a vegetarian menu to cook for me. I discovered he was an excellent cook, and the tortilla we had was delicious.

Over the ensuing months my relationship with Roberto continued to blow hot and cold. My logical brain told me this was emotional suicide; but when I first hugged him the world stopped, my body softened and my heart opened. I felt I was home in a safe harbour. When I let go of Roberto my armour-plated protection would clang shut around me again. Luckily, he was very patient with my Jekyll and Hyde personality. The closer I came to admitting that I loved him deeply, the more fiercely I would pull back defensively.

On meeting Roberto and hearing his history, several of my closest friends challenged my sanity in pursuing this relationship.

"Do you really want to go there again?" Maggie asked me sadly. "I frankly don't think I'm strong enough to endure the pain of watching you losing another partner, Patti."

Yet pursue it I did. I finally understood that it was far better for me to love deeply and with abandon for whatever time was allotted, than to live the rest of my life with a closed heart in fear of loss. Each moment we have to love another is a precious gift.

I fully believe the saying,

> We are not human beings having a spiritual experience;
> We are spiritual beings having a human experience.

We are eternal spirit and Love is eternal, so loss is a misperception. Unfortunately my personality self loses sight of that truth sometimes, and has a hard time agreeing with it.

The irony is that Roberto ended up nursing me, rather than the other way around. Roberto's health improved and all subsequent cancer checks have been clear. I, however, ended up in bed incapacitated for three-and-a-half months. The disc in my neck between cervical 6/7 was pressing on the main nerve into my left arm. I lost all reflexes in that arm and was unable to hold anything in my left hand.

Initially the neurosurgeon took one look at me and booked me in for surgery for the following Monday. Under no circumstances was I to allow anyone to manipulate my neck, as the spinal chord was already being compromised. In the following two days, however, I went to Chris Martinovich, a chiropractor who doesn't do the usual adjustments. He put a linseed poultice on my back for twenty-four hours. It was a relief to feel the spastic muscles protecting my neck begin to relax! The next day Chris used two balls, one the size of a tennis ball and the other like a squash ball, to gently adjust the first few upper thoracic vertebrae. He didn't touch my neck.

When I went back to the surgeon for a pre-operation check he saw that I had marginally improved, so he suggested I recuperate in bed for three-and-a-half months. He said that it was preferable to rest until the disc atrophied enough to take pressure off the nerve, rather than undergo the invasive and risky option of surgery. So to bed I went.

The muscles in my upper back and shoulder would involuntarily contract and I was in constant pain. It felt as if someone was incessantly sawing on the nerves in my neck. I spent most of these months curled on my side in the foetal position with my head stretched to the right to create more space for the nerve. Headaches and nausea were an everyday occurrence over the months that I recuperated. The only place I had less pain was floating in a really hot bath, where Roberto used to hand-feed me with infinite love and patience.

As always, I was beautifully taken care of by family members. Merle, the grandmother of my children, arrived one day with five video tapes of inspiring enlightened women such as Guru Mai and Gangaji. When I was more fully recovered, Merle gave me a copy of *A Cave In The Snow*, an engrossing book about Tenzin Palmo written by Vicki Mackenzie. Even laid low with my life force at one tenth of its normal capacity, the angels were guiding my loved ones to keep me on track.

Once the disc atrophied and I regained the nerve supply to my arm, I used Touch For Health Kinesiology to restore my muscles to full strength.

Roberto was the embodiment of devotion, nurturing and constancy. All doubts about him and our compatibility were erased during this humbling initiation time. I discovered that he was far more open to my perception of life and in sync with my ideologies than I had at first thought. My love, gratitude and respect for Roberto deepened. I said a silent prayer of thanks to Tony; he had indeed sent me a very good man.

*

What a celebration our wedding was. Adam and Craig gave their mum away and Roberto's son Fred was his best man. James and Denise sang accompanied by guitar as I walked down the aisle of the tiny church on Henley Brook. Roberto's daughter Carol and my son Adam did readings for us.

Glowing and blissful, we shared this special ceremony with all the friends and family who had enriched our lives and given it meaning. At the end of the service my godson Sean released twelve enormous monarch butterflies into the church.

At the reception, the Latin American band brought out the extrovert in even the more retiring members of my family. Our Spanish and Argentinean friends always dance at parties, so it was a fun and lively evening. My flower girl Jessica led the group in an uninhibited hip gyrating version of the Makerana. Everyone, including ninety-year-old Alfredo and several staff members, did the limbo under a broom. Instead of a bridal waltz we, of course, did a tango. Everyone danced and danced. In the sweltering thirty-five degree heat of this summer night, Roberto took off his suit jacket and tie, undid his drenched red silk shirt and tied it in a knot at his waist, pirate fashion. We had a ball. It was the best wedding I have been to and I was glad it happened to be mine. The euphoria of the wedding lasted weeks for me.

Rigid Cherished Beliefs

On 20 November 2001, while I was jogging in an aerobics class, I turned and tore my right Achilles tendon. What a noise! It sounded like an old-fashioned pop gun going off. Everyone in the class turned around to see where the loud BANG had come from as I hit the floor clutching my calf in agony.

At the hospital I discovered that I had torn the tendon across and up the length of the fibres. The surgeon likened it to cooked spaghetti and explained that it was very hard to stich the strands back on.

After surgery to reattach the muscles, my leg was put in a cast. I was instructed to not put any weight on it, even with the cast on. This meant I couldn't do much at all. In fact, the only thing I could do was sit at the computer with my leg propped up, and start writing this book. My guides had been urging me for the previous couple of years to put my experiences that were in journal form, into a book. I still doubted my ability to do this so chose to ignore them.

An angelic guide who called himself Raphael was assigned to me to assist me through the process. Like Archangel Michael, Raphael appeared to me as a column of light, with the ghostly outline of a human form to make it easier to converse with him. Raphael manifested with shoulder-length hair and a gentle, bearded face, wearing a loose robe, whereas Michael was clean-shaven.

The angels are non-physical and tend to manifest to humans in whatever form is easiest for their belief systems to handle. I had the sense that the angels I was conversing with were individualized expressions of the group consciousness blue light beings.

I managed to busy myself during the day and avoid writing, so Raphael would shake me awake at three in the morning.

"You may as well get up, Patti," he hassled me. "I am not going to let you go back to sleep, so get up and write!" If not for the injury and Raphael pestering me, I would be still procrastinating about writing this book.

Finally, six weeks later, it was time to take the cast off. Hooray! Over the next few days I noticed that my leg turned deep purple from the knee down within thirty seconds of standing up. Further investigation revealed that I had deep vein thrombosis in two veins from mid-calf to the top of the back of my knee. So back into hospital for a few days to have that sorted out. While I was in hospital Raphael materialized in the corner of the room. He put on a surgical mask, symbolically indicating that more surgery was to come. I thought, "You've got to be kidding!"

I was sent home again with orders for complete bed rest, which I was happy to comply with. Two days later Diane came to visit me. She and Roberto became distressed at my inability to understand what they were saying, or to respond coherently to them. My breathing was strange, as I couldn't seem to get enough air into my lungs, and I couldn't think straight. I was whisked back into hospital for chest x-rays. Raphael appeared in the corner and took off his surgical mask, so I knew that they wouldn't find anything in the x-ray: which they didn't.

When I was back in my hospital bed, Raphael reappeared in his favourite corner holding a syringe. He put his surgical mask back on. It turned out that another chest scan was ordered, which involved my being injected with radioactive isotopes. Because Raphael had put the mask back on I knew they would find something. The scans revealed a spray of small pulmonary embolisms in both lungs.

Raphael appeared and asked me if I wanted to stay alive or go. I was surprised that I had a choice. I was unfazed by the idea of dying; it hadn't occurred to me that my body was in any danger. I said telepathically to him, "If there is more for me to do and learn I would prefer to stay. I also wouldn't mind sticking around to see my sons married and have children."

Bev drove from Nannup, four hours from Perth, to Bunbury, two hours from Perth, to pick up Maggie. They then drove to Mandurah to collect Diane. The three of them arrived in my hospital room demanding an explanation.

"What on earth do you think you are doing, Patti?" Maggie's internal radar had picked up that I might be checking out.

"I'm fine, guys. I'm not going anywhere. You're stuck with me for quite a while yet," I reassured my darling buddies.

The doctors stabilized my blood-thinning medication and sent me home again.

As the weeks progressed the reminder of further surgery from Raphael was forgotten. I taught my first Brain Gym class on crutches. It was great to be back at work after so much inactivity. At the end of the second day I locked up my clinic and headed for the car park.

I tripped ever so slightly on uneven ground and felt a sickening *"fffft"* in my heel as the tendon gave way once more. This time there was no pop; nothing was holding it together at all. The stitches had dissolved before any significant healing had taken place, because of the extensive clots clogging my veins. Blood poured out through the scar, spoiling the sexy white TED stockings I wore for the thrombosis. The pain the second time around was unbelievable. When the ambulance man asked me what was my pain out of ten, my reply was, "Fifteen!"

It was disconcerting how accurate Raphael was. The nurses did a double-take when they saw me back for the fourth time within a few months! The weird thing was I kept being given the same room with the same picture to stare at. It was a little too much like the movie *Groundhog Day* for comfort.

Keyhole surgery using permanent stitches was tried this time, to minimize the trauma and bleeding into my leg. When I came to, I was in a cast for the second time. I informed the nurses and doctors that the outside of my foot was numb and I got shooting nerve pains down past my ankle into my foot when I sat up. The consensus was that the nerves were disturbed from the trauma, but that it would settle down.

When Raphael once more put on a surgical mask, I rolled away from him in disgust. The thought of more surgery was too much to bear. A few days later I was sent home again. The numbness in my foot increased until the whole foot was involved. At night I would be woken up by shooting pains when I moved in the wrong direction. Finally, in desperation I rang the doctor.

For the fifth time I went into hospital; this time I specifically asked for a different room in the hope of breaking the jinx. The nerve feeding the side of my foot had been sewn up with one of the stitches and needed to be released. Six more weeks in a cast followed this operation. It took eight months to regrow the nerve down the outside of my foot.

*

What a comedown after a lifetime of good health, vitality and physical fitness! In the last three years I had spent almost eight months in bed or incapacitated.

My body seemed to take a long time to heal from both the neck and the Achilles tendon injuries. I continued to experience weakness, numbness, and neuralgia up into my whole face and down both arms, on and off for a further eighteen months. Roberto had suggested it was because I was a vegetarian that I wasn't fully recovering. Of course, I poo-pooed the idea as my health had been great for so long. Then he came home from work with a story about an athlete who became a vegetarian and then tore his Achilles tendon. Roberto heard two similar stories in the same week. I was not listening. Eating meat was not an option for me because I was an ideological vegetarian. I chose not to eat meat as I didn't want to be responsible for the unnecessary death of an animal. I ate free range unfertilised eggs and dairy products, but no meat or seafood.

I felt so nagged by Roberto's repeated pleas to consider the meat option that I went to see Wynelle. She dowsed that for the last eight years my body's metabolism had been slowly deteriorating as it was unable to get enough protein from vegetables alone. In short, my body needed animal protein. Wynelle suggested that deep sea fish would be best. I still was not convinced.

I asked two vegetarian female friends for their input. They both said that like me they had felt great their entire adult lives on a vegetarian diet. As soon as they hit menopause, however, their energy had dropped and they started eating fish to regain their vitality. So maybe my age was a factor, combined with the fact that I was still trying to exercise as if I was a twenty-five-year-old.

"I read somewhere that the Dalai Lama has to eat meat for health reasons, Patti", Diane said encouragingly.

"Yes, I have heard that," I grudgingly replied.

"And have you seen the *Eat Right for Your Blood Type* book?" Susie added.

"Yes, yes," I testily responded. "I'm an O type and I know that O positive blood types are meant to eat red meat according to the book. It doesn't make it any easier to do, though."

Finally I succumbed and started eating deep sea fish such as Red Emperor. Tears streamed down my face, and I had a tension headache eating my first fish. I felt I had betrayed all my ideals. I was a very sorry sight to watch for the first half a dozen meals. My internal conflict was enormous. Within two weeks I had to admit my energy was much higher. Roberto then started pushing me to eat red meat. I was having none of it. In my mind I had gone against my principles enough already.

Numbness and neuralgia in both sides of my face and head and down both arms persisted. The neurosurgeon ordered more tests, as he believed the problem was no longer relating to my neck and he wanted to rule out the possibility of a brain tumour. After a barrage of brain scans, blood tests and nerve function tests, nothing conclusive showed up. This was a great relief and a source of frustration because we were none the wiser as to what was causing the problem.

The specialist doing the nerve function tests for my arms asked me out of the blue, "Are you a vegetarian?"

"Yes. Why do you ask?" I queried.

"The whites of you eyes are blue, which suggests that you are anaemic."

This was one more person telling me that I needed animal protein.

In desperation I tried eating red meat. It was even harder than eating fish. Surprise, surprise! After only two weeks of eating red meat all symptoms completely vanished. Two months later my health and my energy were fully restored for the first time in years.

This was one of the hardest decisions I have ever made. It was a pity I had to be virtually on my knees with ill health in order to make the necessary changes. One of my most rigid and cherished beliefs had finally been shattered.

Planetary Healing

With my newfound energy came more crystal healing work. Patricia arrived from Queensland to teach a Flower Of Life Workshop at my clinic and to do dolphin healing research at Bunbury. It was wonderful to connect again.

At the end of the workshop the group agreed to do a planetary healing meditation with me. I shared my story about following guidance and placing crystals around Australia to stabilize the coastline. We constructed an imaginary map of Australia in the room, and I invited the eleven participants to place themselves at whatever landmark they were drawn to go to.

To my surprise they didn't elect to spread out, one person to an individual site. Six people gathered at Denmark, in the south of Western Australia; three at Adelaide, South Australia; one with me at Kata Tjuta (Olgas), Central Australia; and one in Queensland.

I found this spread of people very interesting because while my leg was in plaster I was guided to do many healing meditations for the Earth in the sea floor one thousand nautical miles south off the coast of Denmark. It related to resolving old Lemurian patterns of abuse of power. The fact that half the group chose to hold the energy at that place let me know that the work there was continuing. (I hadn't told them that I had been doing work in that area).

I enjoy the added power and focus of group healing work. The crystals were energised and aligned, then all the points were connected to each other by energy lines. Particular focus was given to the lines up the west coast of Australia, from Darwin through the centre (Olgas) to Adelaide, and from Monkey Mia across to Mt Beerwah in Queensland. Finally the nodal points off the coast were activated. Love and gratitude were sent down into Mother Earth and up to Father Sky. We then sent love and healing to the whole planet.

The next day Patricia received a phone call from her friend Richie, who lives on a catamaran near Hervey Bay in Queensland. Richie spends his time placing crystals around Australia in triangular connecting grids to amplify the energy, and communing with the whales and dolphins at Hervey Bay.

"Patti, Richie just said that yesterday a new line of energy was set up running from Monkey Mia to near Maleny." He picked up on the work that our group was doing! That's not all. He said Spirit wants him to go to a place called Denmark in WA. He asked if I knew where that was."

I love having confirmation like that, from people on the other side of the country whom I had never met.

*

Patricia gave Richie my phone number and vice versa. I thought it would be great to meet him if he did come to Perth sometime. True to his commitment to following Spirit, he flew to Perth a few months later. I explained to Richie that my work schedule was too full to go to Monkey Mia with him, but that I could spare a few days to go down south to Denmark.

The week before the trip I attended a Kinesiology Practitioners' day. During morning tea break I chatted with Irene about my doing a trip to Denmark to do some Earth healing and place a crystal. Irene is a Kinesiologist and spiritualist minister who makes her own powerful Innate Healing Flower Essences. "The crystal needs to be placed near the Petrified Forest," she advised.

"I've never heard of it. Where is it?"

"It's near William Bay outside Denmark. What's more, I think I need to come too! I want to make some more essences with flowers from that area."

At that point another lady joined our conversation. "When you're in Denmark go to the Petrified Forest. It's a really special place."

I laughed, "Well, it looks like the Petrified Forest is on the agenda then."

Roberto volunteered to drive Irene, Richie and me down south. Although a storm warning had been issued we decided to go anyway. The trip down was very windy, but we didn't encounter much rain. We went to the chalets in Peaceful Bay and lit a cosy fire.

The next morning was overcast and grey with buffeting winds, huge sea swells and intermittent showers. After a group meditation and thanksgiving on the beach we drove to Conspicuous Cliffs in the Walpole-Nornalup National Park. It couldn't have looked more desolate. A recent fire had ravaged the bush right down to the ocean, and the wooden stairway to the beach was burnt out. One area which was intact was the whale watching platform. Braving the elements, Irene and I meditated there for guidance, then compared notes. I was told that there was a composite of four flowers that we had to make up. We knew already what two of the flowers were. Irene had spotted them on the drive into the area: Tea Tree and Swamp Bottlebrush.

It started to rain again, so we scrambled into the car and headed for the Tingle forest, which was Richie's next port of call. On the way Irene noticed the four flowers she needed for the combination essence, all growing in the one spot. The rain held off long enough for her to harvest them. The essence they were made into is used to bring out the qualities of leadership and the ability to inspire and lead others. The combination was named Conspicuous Cliffs after the area they were found in.

It was soothing and grounding to spend some time amongst the magnificent Tingle trees with the unusually shaped and brightly coloured fungi at their bases. The next stop was William Bay, to find the Petrified Forest. We scrub-bashed and tried to access it, but all the old bush tracks were barred, and it was proving too far to walk there and back in the remaining daylight.

"If we can't get to the petrified trees then the place for the crystal must be near by," I said. "All the crystals I have placed are near water and rocks. The rocks right at William Bay aren't appropriate because it is such a public place."

"Let's go for a drive and look around," Irene suggested.

We climbed back into the car and headed towards the ocean, then went left up a bush track. "There!" I pointed. "Those are the rocks I have to go to. I just know it. That one shaped like an ice cream cone looks like a beacon to me."

Irene and Richie stayed in the car while Roberto and I attempted to find a path to the two rocks sticking out above the scrub. We followed our noses down overgrown tracks. After about ten minutes of walking I saw a young male Aboriginal spirit on one of the rocky hills that we passed. This was the first spirit I had seen on this trip, so I knew we were in the right area.

It proved to be much further to the rocks than I thought. I was like a bloodhound following a juicy scent. Roberto asked me repeatedly to turn back as we would be walking back in the dark. I finally agreed he was right, so we returned to the car and to Cosy Corner for dinner.

The next morning Richie and I decided that we would go to the rocks and do a joint ceremony. We had a lovely walk and instinctively took the right path with no need to backtrack. As we got closer we could see there were actually three main rocks reaching skywards. One was the pointy ice cream cone. To its right was a huge rock which looked like the profile of an extraterrestrial, shaped like the high-domed, backward-sloping skulls found in South America and in the early Egyptian pharaohs. Between them was the smallest outcrop.

Richie and I asked out loud for permission from the spirits of the land to enter the rock site and do our work. We both toned while I played my Tibetan singing bowl, and we cleared the space and called in angelic, devic and ancestral Aboriginal guardian support for our work. Richie meditated and did his own internal process while I did mine. As all of the Galactic wands had been placed long ago, I brought with me a smoky quartz with sand grains in it. I reconnected with the crystalline point of light in the sea with the help of the whales. My guides asked me to reactivate the highest and best aspects of the Lemurian thought patterns and culture:

- Group consciousness and telepathy.

- Peace, love and harmony working in groups.

- Ability for groups to focus with one mind and heart into crystals which in turn amplified and focused the energy. This created etheric vibrational networks that strengthened the Earth and humanity by maintaining health, fertility and harmony.

- Vibrational healing using sound.

As I focused on bringing this vibration through, the pointy rock lit up etherically like a beacon. When I opened my eyes Richie had created a beautiful nature altar out of special shells, water and crystals collected from sacred places around Australia and the world. He put a casing of small rocks around so that it would be hidden and protected. Richie said a beautiful prayer and blessing, then we quietly walked back to Irene and Roberto.

The four of us held hands and reconnected with the light energy created at the rocks. We asked once more for permission from the indigenous spirit guardians of the land and Song Lines to send this healing to the rest of Australia.

I called out the places where the Galactic wands had been placed, then Richie named all the places around Australia he had activated crystals. In my mind's eye I saw a web of light crisscrossing the continent connecting them all as our combined positive intentions and prayers united.

"Now that it's all over, Patti," Irene said, "I want to tell you something as confirmation for you. I didn't want to influence your choices, so I kept quiet until now." I looked at her expectantly. "A psychic woman whom I greatly respect once told me that those rocks are the record keepers of the Lemurian consciousness."

On the way home to Perth we drove past my old home in Torbay. It was wonderful to see that the hundreds of trees I had helped to plant had grown so tall and lush that I could hardly see the house. This was the place where my adventure had started fifteen years ago. It is refreshing to know that my original idea that my body is like a crystal and can be cleansed and realigned with my focused, consistent intention, is not so crazy after all.

Dr. Masaru Emoto's research in *Messages from Water* shows us that when prayers, loving thoughts or words are focused on water, the water takes on those vibrations. If that water is frozen and photographed using an electron microscope, beautiful crystalline structures can be seen. When negative thoughts, words or polluted feelings are focused into water, the water loses its crystalline structure and harmony.

Seventy-five percent of our bodies consist of water. It makes sense to maintain beautiful crystalline structures of health and vitality within ourselves, each other and the world by holding love and gratitude in our hearts and using our positive intention to consciously co-create reality with our minds.

Does that mean we have to be perfect? Hell no. Who is? For me, life is a continual challenge, urging me to reassess my beliefs, and let go of my prejudices, negativity and limitations. I do this by forgiving myself and others when we fall short of my ideals and using any techniques that help me to return to a path of greater joy and grace. I give thanks to all the human crystals in my life who love and support me in spite of my shortcomings, and who value and celebrate our differences.

Epilogue

"Please light a candle and meditate," Raphael telepathically instructed. Once I was in a peaceful meditative state, I asked Raphael why they had wanted me to write *Human Crystals*.

"It is our intention with *Human Crystals* to activate in the reader a desire for a sense of purpose beyond everyday life.

"Your next book, *Soul Braiding*, will assist people to find their higher life purpose."

Soul Braiding: *bringing the soul to Light*

- Individual Soul Braiding of your highest purpose.
- Soul Braiding of our interdimensional angelic selves.
- Soul Group Braiding.

*

Patricia Leahy-Shrewsbury grew up in the country on the Narrogin Agricultural School where her father Ted Leahy was a teacher and farm supervisor. Her love of the land and the environment was instilled in her childhood where she spent her free time playing in the bush, exploring fox holes along the creek, mushrooming and listening to the wind whispering in the casuarina trees.

Patricia now lives in Perth, Western Australia with her husband Roberto. She is director of the WA Kinesiology Centre where she consults and teaches Kinesiology and her own work; Cellular Memory Integration.